D0417678

Clapham
Dissenters

Clapham Dissenters

From Persecuted Group to Prestigious Congregation

IVOR THOMAS REES

First impression: 2015

© Copyright Ivor Thomas Rees and Y Lolfa Cyf., 2015

The contents of this book are subject to copyright, and may not
be reproduced by any means, mechanical or electronic, without
the prior, written consent of the publishers.

Cover image reproduced by permission of
London Borough of Lambeth, Archives Department

lambethlandmark.com

To the author's best knowledge, the copyright for photographs
of W. Morton Barwell and Leslie Artingstall originally belonged
to the Congregational Union and passed to the United Reformed
Church (URC) as their legal successor. These images are both used
with the permission of the URC. However, if you have knowledge
of another individual or organisation claiming copyright for this
material, please contact the publisher.

ISBN: 978 1 78461 076 0

Published and printed in Wales
on paper from well-maintained forests by
Y Lolfa Cyf., Talybont, Ceredigion SY24 5HE
website www.ylolfa.com
e-mail ylolfa@ylolfa.com
tel 01970 832 304
fax 832 782

Contents

BOOKS BY IVOR THOMAS REES

Welsh Hustings 1885–2004 (2005)

Yr Wythnos Honno (2011)

Saintly Enigma (2011)

Pathway to the Cross (2012)

The Sledgehammer Pastor (2015)

Foreword

IN RECENT TIMES historians have been keen to remind us that there is such a thing as local history. Events and people have significance in their own context, and the propensity to reach general conclusions from specific and localised events too quickly should be avoided. What happens, wherever it happens, is important for its own sake. Having said this, it is also clear that such work often has wider resonance. Patterns emerge that can be identified in other places, either during the same or during other periods. This book succeeds in highlighting both aspects: for the history of Clapham's Dissenters is in some sense the history of English Nonconformity, while the history of Clapham is mirrored in many other communities throughout Britain.

In this book Ivor Rees discusses how a village became a suburb and how a church was established along Independent lines in the 1640s. He recounts how the Dissenters survived the direct persecution of the Clarendon Code to grow in number, confidence and influence by the mid-nineteenth century, when they built and opened their ostentatious, cathedral-like chapel (destroyed by Nazi bombs rather than the secularism which caused the demise of so many other places of worship during the twentieth century). He outlines the life and contribution of ministers and members who lived through the heyday of Nonconformity as well as the subsequent decline in numbers and the development of a more outward-looking and ecumenical ministry in the twentieth century until the church finally closed its doors in 2002. He knew the church and the area well, having ministered there himself. The story is in some senses unique; it belongs to this particular place and to these particular people. And yet the narrative framework is easily applied elsewhere. This is not (thankfully) a book which tries to teach lessons. It is not an account of why this happened, but instead that it did so. And that, in itself, is a tale worth telling.

Revd Dr Robert Pope

Preface

THOUGH I CLAIM not be sentimental about either the closure of church buildings in general or the end of a particular cause when its work is done, I was deeply saddened by the news that Clapham Congregational Church had closed its doors. Its remaining members had moved in faith to witness Christ and unite with St Andrew's United Reformed Church across Clapham Common.

Founded in 1645, if not 1640 as some church records put it, its story is a microcosm of the history of English Protestant dissent. Apart from the memories of a few elderly members, the congregation which welcomed me so warmly in 1967 had few links with the south London 'cathedral' of pre-war days; many of the members had little formal church background and even less interest in history. They told me that 'everything had been destroyed in the old building by the last V2 of the war.'

Then, a local historian, Mr Eric E. F. Smith, secretary of the Clapham Antiquarian Society, published a fine book, *Clapham; an historical tour* (1968). In reply to my letter regretting the absence of any reference to the Congregational church in the book, Mr Smith asked for permission to see the Minute Book for 1773 and other documents. Once more my enquiries were fruitless, until one day the caretaker produced a large black metal box containing a treasure-trove of historical material, including the Minute Book and large quantities of eighteenth-, nineteenth- and early twentieth-century letters. Those letters from the first two centuries, written in exquisite Jane Austen-style English, often said the most unpleasant things about fellow church members. There were also carbon copies of letters typed by the minister, Edward W. Lewis, during the first decade of the twentieth century. The Minute Book, together with the minutes of deacons' meetings and other materials, has now been deposited at the London Metropolitan Archives, while some copies of *Grafton News*, the church magazine, are lodged at the Lambeth Archives. Sadly, several decades of the church magazine and some personal letters appear to be lost, but the history of the church, *A History of Clapham Congregational Church*, written by F. Reynolds Lovett in 1912, remains, as does *What we are doing at Grafton Square* published by the church in 1912 as well.

***

My thanks must go especially to Miss Hazel Smith, one of the few remaining members of the Clapham church, both for her invaluable help and for saving many of the church's precious records. Also thanks to Ms Alyson Whyte of the Clapham Society for her aid and encouragement.

I received valued assistance from Mr John Henderson of Lambeth Archives, the staff of London Metropolitan Archives, and Dr David Powell from London's Congregational Library.

The reminiscences of other former ministers of the church: the Revds Ann Maureen Cole, Egland Graham, Alex Mabbs and the late Olive Symes, added greatly to the telling of the story. Sadly, the Revd Mary Read of Ewell was unable to contribute because of ill health, but she too should be thanked for her great work at Clapham church as well as the support given by her and husband Professor Jim Read to me when I was minister at Ewell in Surrey

The helpful advice of the Revd Dr Alan Sell, the Revd Professor David M. Thompson and Mrs Margaret Thomas was much appreciated. I am grateful to Dr Jean Silvan-Evans for her suggestions as to the content, and to the Revd Dr Robert Pope for his meticulous reading of the manuscript and valued advice, and for writing the foreword.

Thanks for permission to quote go to Professor David W. Bebbington from his *The Nonconformist Conscience: Chapel and Politics 1870–1914* (1982) and to the family of the late Professor R. Tudur Jones from his *Congregationalism in England* (1962). Some of the material contained in this book is held at the London Metropolitan Archives and I am grateful to the archive and to the Revd Robert Rominger (General Secretary, 2008–14) on behalf of the United Reformed Church for their permission to make use of this material.

The matter of the copyright of Dr G. Stanley Russell's autobiography *The Road Behind Me* (1936) proved to be complicated. Dr Stanley died in 1974 and was predeceased by his wife. They had no children. The book's publisher is no longer in business. The Macmillan companies of the UK and USA had no information, nor had John Wiley and Sons, who took over some of Macmillan Canada's titles. My thanks for their assistance with copyright permission goes to Tina Lusignan, Registry Officer, Copyright Board of Canada and Ms Jessica Luet, Research Specialist Access Copyright of the Canadian Copyright Licensing Agency, as well as the Canadian Intellectual Property Office. Mr John Hurley of the UK Intellectual Property Office receives the same thanks. As far as can be ascertained, *The Road Behind Me* was not published in the UK and thus is not subject to UK regulation.

As is always the case, my greatest thanks go to my wife Delyth for her constant encouragement and support, as well as for her usual careful reading of the manuscript and helpful comments.

Clapham Dissenters played a major role in the story of Protestant Nonconformity in England and Wales, and their tale needs to be told. My hope is that this contribution, based on articles written by me for the church magazine *Grafton News*, and from reading *A History of Clapham Congregational Church* and *What we are doing at Grafton Square*, will encourage a genuine church historian to give this story the attention it deserves. I regret that much of the story concentrates on ministers but this is due to the difficulty in obtaining material about other people, especially in the earlier centuries. In the meantime I commend this fascinating story to its readers, with my thanks to God for being allowed to share a little in one of its finest periods.

Ivor Thomas Rees
May 2015

1

Beginnings

SCHOOLCHILDREN IN WALES, as in England, used to be taught
– perhaps they still are – that the English Reformation came
about because the King of England wanted to divorce his wife.
What followed was political. It was set against the European
understanding of *Cuius regio, eius religio* (Whose realm, his
religion), that to differ from the ruler in anything, including
religion, endangered the state.

Thus it was Henry VIII and Elizabeth I who created the
English (and Welsh) Reformation by establishing the Church
of England, while on Continental Europe the Reformation
is associated with names like Luther, Calvin and Zwingli. It
is worth noting that the Reformation in England and Wales
produced far more martyrs, both Protestant and Catholic,
than did its continental version in the period between Martin
Luther nailing his ninety-five theses to the doors of the church
at Wittenberg, and the death of John Calvin in 1564.

It should be noted, too, that the primary concern of the
English monarchs, apart from Mary Tudor, was the safety of
the realm, and religious conformity was only and element of
this. The official settlement is, of course, but a part of the story.
The British Isles was not cut off from continental thought, and
ideas spread.

Religious dissent raised its head from time to time during the
Middle Ages, and the invention of printing turned a trickle into
a river of ideas. Anabaptist congregations appeared in Europe –
the followers of Thomas Müntzer at Wittenberg, the Hutterites

of Moravia, together with similar groups in Switzerland and Holland. Their vision was of a Church completely separated from the world, with no compromise to either state authority or secular values. They abhorred all established churches, Catholic or Protestant. Separatist fellowships appeared, mainly in London, though little is known of them. The only time they spoke of themselves was when they were summoned before ecclesiastical authorities.

On 19 June 1567 the sheriffs of London went to the Plumbers' Hall where they found a congregation of about a hundred people gathered for worship. The minister and a number of other people were arrested, and they appeared next day before the Lord Mayor and the Bishop of London and other dignitaries. This is the first recorded separatist congregation. Later, a group of Cambridge graduates of separatist views began to write and preach. Prominent among them was Robert Browne (1550–1633), an alumnus of Corpus Christi College. Browne, with Robert Harrison, another alumnus of the college, gathered a church based on Congregational principles in Norwich in 1580. After Browne was arrested and then released, they moved the church to Middelburg in the Netherlands, where it organised itself on New Testament principles and was known for its semi-separation. But, within two years, it had been riven asunder by internal dissensions. In 1585 Browne returned home and entered holy orders in the Church of England. He was sent to Northampton prison for assaulting a constable and died there. Robert Harrison died in Middelburg in 1585 of a broken heart, or so it is said.

Despite the brevity of his separatist activity (1579–85), Browne is regarded as the father of English Congregationalism, especially so because of the two books written by him: *A Treatise of Reformation without Tarying for Anie*, in which he set out the right of the church to effect necessary reforms without the authorisation of the civil magistrate, and also *A Booke which sheweth the life and manners of all True Christians*, which contained the theory of Congregational independency. Both were published in Middelburg in 1582. The cost of dissent is revealed in the fact that, in 1583, two men were hanged in Bury St Edmunds for circulating the books.

The reign of Elizabeth I was threatened from within and outside her realm. To reject church order established by the queen was seen as treason, whether it be by a Catholic or a Protestant dissenter. Separatists met in London, and among them was Henry Barrow, a courtier turned Puritan, who withdrew into private life. His friend John Greenwood and others were arrested when worshiping in the house of Henry Martin on 8 October 1586, and Greenwood was taken to Clink prison. On a visit to see him, Barrow himself was arrested. Both were transferred to Fleet prison in May 1587 where they were subjected to a series of examinations before judges before being brought to trial. They were executed on 6 April 1593.

By the end of 1590, some 52 separatists were in London prisons but, despite a reign of terror, Puritans remained active. A new separatist church was formed in 1592 and within six months there were 72 members. Among them was a newcomer, John Penry, a Welshman from Breconshire and a graduate of both Oxford and Cambridge. In 1587, concerned at the need for the evangelising of Wales, he submitted three treatises to Parliament, the first being *Aequity of an Humble Supplication*. He is also believed to have been a contributor to the *Marprelate Tracts*, if not the author. A charge of sedition was brought against him, based on a draft petition to the queen. He was hanged on 29 May 1593.

The previous month had seen the passing of an Act to retain the queen's subjects in obedience. So, the London separatists left the country, and settled in Amsterdam. Internal dissension led to the secession of a large group of members in 1610. Some of the remainder sailed to Virginia in 1618, with many dying of fever mid-Atlantic.

The accession of James I to the English throne led Puritans to expect an improvement in their lot, but they were soon disabused. The king's hostility to their position was made clear

15

in the Canons of 1603. The Canons followed on from *The Thirty-Nine Articles of Religion* of 1563 and were concerned with the order of worship and, in particular, the administering of Holy Communion. Incumbents of livings were to remind their flocks of their duty to be present at the sacrament, and not to pass this responsibility on to curates. The sacrament was to be regularly celebrated; parishioners were to be present 'oftentimes' and 'at least thrice in the year', while members of universities and cathedrals should attend at least four times.

Several incumbents were deprived of their livings in 1605. Nevertheless, John Smyth gathered a new church in Gainsborough in 1606 and John Robinson in Scrooby and Richard Bernard in Worksop in the same year. Persecution led Smyth and Robinson to go to the Netherlands, where Smyth became a Baptist. Robinson moved with his people to Leiden in southern Holland where they suffered little persecution and he was not troubled by the bitterness of the older separatists. Although his *Justification of Separatism* (1610) set out that case, Robinson acknowledged that the grace of God could be at work within the Church of England, despite its false constitution. His *Of Religious Communion Public and Private* (1614) declared that a refusal to share in the official life of the Church of England did not prevent sharing in godly acts with individual Anglicans. Around 1617 he stated that separatists could attend parish churches to hear godly preachers expound the Christian message.

John Robinson's people took these principles to Cape Cod. They were also applied in London by his friend Henry Jacob when he founded the Independent Church in Southwark in 1616. It was this kind of dissent that appeared at the Clapham church.

Despite the legal obstacles in its way, Puritanism grew during the reigns of James I and Charles I, as Puritans sought the further reformation of the church. By 1640, the year of the calling of the Long Parliament, England was broadly divided between Anglican Royalists and Puritans. Most of the latter were Presbyterian.

Parliament convened an Assembly of Divines at Westminster during the First Civil War (1642–6), whose role was to formulate a new church order for England. Its 151 members could be divided into Episcopal, Erastian, Presbyterian and Dissenting groups. The Presbyterians had an absolute majority but were opposed by the 'Dissenting Brethren'. It was in their own statement, the 'Apologeticall Narration' that the word 'Congregational' first appears to represent a distinctive church polity.

With the close of the Civil War(s) and the establishment of the Commonwealth, Independency gained power through the person of the Lord Protector, Oliver Cromwell. By 1660, the year of the restoration of the monarchy, it had matured greatly. As shall be seen, Dissenters made a point of welcoming the new monarch to his throne but the now-triumphant Royalists were determined to return to the old ecclesiastical order, and equally determined to punish Dissenters.

2

Clapham, the Place

JOHN BATTLEY'S SIXPENNY *Clapham Guide* of 1935 tells us that the derivation of the name is uncertain but refers 'to one of the earliest records of the district' and its account of the feast given by Osgod Clapha, a Saxon noble, to celebrate the wedding of his daughter Gytha to Tovi the Proud at his 'ham' (homestead) at Lambeth (Lambi's landing place on the river bank). During the celebrations King Harthacanute suffered a fit and died some days later at Clapha's Ham.

Some time after the Norman Conquest the manor of Clapham was held by the family of Geoffrey de Manneville for several generations. After having several other owners, it was purchased by Dr Henry Atkyns, physician to James I, remaining in the hands of his family until 1795. To inherit the estate, Richard Bowker added Atkyns and the manor was certainly in the possession of the Atkyns-Bowker family in 1935.

A parish church was built by Merton Priory in the twelfth century on the site of the present St Paul's, Clapham, but was replaced as Clapham's parish church by Holy Trinity, 'the church on the Common' in 1775. When the author arrived in 1967, Clapham had become five parishes, two of which could be called Anglo-Catholic and one Evangelical. It was only the last of these which did not share in any inter-church or ecumenical activity or, indeed, have much to do with its Anglican neighbours.

The 'Calendar of Close Rolls' for 1326 informs us that the population of the manor consisted of the lord and his household, about three freemen, 31 bondmen and four cottars, who held a dwelling and a small piece of land in return for certain services to the lord. It may be assumed that there would have been some 200 residents on manor land, together with another 150 within the parish but outside the manor boundaries.

Mid-sixteenth-century registers reveal that the population remained small, for in the ten years between 1551 and 1561 there were only eleven marriages, twelve baptisms and 24 funerals. A century later (1651–61), there were 61 marriages, 103 baptisms and 113 funerals. This growth continued throughout the next century: the decade 1751–61 saw 88 marriages, 220 baptisms and 399 funerals. The plague hit the village in 1603 and 1665, when whole families were wiped out. In 1665 the churchwardens spent £21-7-0 on building a 'Pest House' in which to isolate infected people who were nursed by Goodwife Gurney, who received £5-8-0 for nine weeks' nursing. The churchwardens' accounts in the seventeenth and eighteenth centuries contain many references to the poor of the parish, and the small sums given to those who could prove that they were entitled to parish assistance. Poor strangers were driven away and some parish residents were assisted to go and seek help elsewhere. A poorhouse was built in 1722, enlarged in 1732, and converted in a workhouse in 1745. A doctor was employed to care for the poor on a salary of £5-5-0 per annum in 1738. Pauper children were farmed out to 'goodwives' in the parish, with some boys and girls being bound to be apprentices from 1668. In 1812 a chimney sweeping machine was purchased to remove the need for climbing-boys.

The first 'watch' was appointed when a watch-house was built in 1690. That year saw the first daily stagecoach service to Gracechurch Street in the City. Roads were bad and highwaymen busy. The Windmill tavern on the Common was reputed to have been a haunt of Dick Turpin. The last hold-up took place in 1801.

Parish church records refer to payments for 'the killing of

polecats and hedgehogs'. A committee was set up in 1768 to prevent residents from taking over common land. In 1796, the parish beadle announced that a free cart would be sent around each Saturday morning in order to prevent the throwing of ashes and rubbish on the Common, and the material would be used to fill up dangerous holes there.

David Hughson, in his *History of London* (1808), describes Clapham as a village about four miles from Westminster Bridge, and consisting of:

> ... many handsome houses, surrounding a common that commands many pleasing views. This common about the commencement of the present reign, was little better than a morass, and the roads were almost impassable. The latter are now in an excellent state, and the common so beautifully planted with trees, that it has the appearance of a park. These improvements were effected by a subscription of the inhabitants, who, on this occasion, have been much indebted to the taste and exertions of Mr Christopher Baldwin, for many years an inhabitant, and an active magistrate; and as a proof of the consequent increased value of property on this spot, Mr Baldwin has sold fourteen acres of land near his own house for £5,000. A reservoir near the Wandsworth Road supplies the village with water. The Common, still about 220 acres in extent, is bounded on the eastern side by Balham Hill Road, which is a continuation of the road through Newington on the north-west by Battersea Rise; and on the south-west by a roadway, dotted at intervals with private residences standing within their own grounds, and 'embosomed high in tufted trees'. Like Peckham Rye, and such other open spaces of the kind as are left in the suburbs of London, Clapham Common in its time has had its fair share of patronage, either of those who delight in the healthful and invigorating game of cricket, or of those who desire a quiet stroll over its velvet-like turf. Pleasure-fairs, too, were held here on Good Friday, Easter and Whit Mondays, and on 'Derby Day'; but these were abolished in 1873. The Common is ornamented with a few large ponds, which add not a little to the charm of the place.

The Chertsey Register from the reign of Alfred names

it 'Clappenham', while in the *Doomsday Book* it is called 'Clopeham'. Water was obtained from a well on North Side, supplied by an ancient spring. Another well across the road came into use in 1789 and supplied the village until 1825. Demand grew with increased population and people living nearby complained about the queues of men with their carts waiting their turn. A subscription paid for a larger well, 100 yards away on the Common, became 'the source of employment and support to 18 families'.[1]

Clapham Common was not always a place of peace in the eighteenth century, not least because its area was divided between the parishes of Clapham and Battersea. This led to many disputes, culminating in a crisis when the lord of the manor of Battersea, Lord St John, ordered the building of a bank and fence, with a ditch, across the western half of the Common. The men of Clapham attacked it and the matter went to law. Clapham won the case, but the Battersea men continued to protest. By the end of the century the Common had been drained, roads repaired and trees planted. It was regarded as a 'healthy place' with breezes on the higher ground, safe from the diseases of the river.

Its proximity to the City and the development of transport links made it a most attractive place to live. The growth of Clapham as a residential district had started in the second half of the seventeenth century. Magnificent houses began to appear, especially on the Common's North Side. Samuel Pepys lived at the residence of his friend William Hewer for the last three years of his life, until his death in 1703. The eighteenth century saw the building of many gracious dwellings, especially in the period 1775–1825, for both members of the aristocracy and, increasingly, for wealthy London merchants.

Among the people who built houses in Clapham were the Hon. John Elliot, brother-in-law of both Prime Minister William Pitt and William Wilberforce; Sir Charles Trevelyan; Thomas Astle, antiquary and Keeper of the Records at the

Tower of London; and John Walter, founder of *The Times*. Mrs Elizabeth Cook, widow of Captain Cook, was a resident, as were H. Bromley Derry, Master of the King's Music; John Francis Bentley, architect of Westminster Cathedral; John Jebb, Bishop of Limerick; Henry Twining, tea merchant; and the Lord Mayor of London, Sir John Barnard. It is clear from the autobiography of Congregational minister, Dr J. Guinness Rogers, that this gentrification of Clapham was reflected in the attendees not only of the parish church but also of the Congregational church.

By 1828 there were eight houses receiving thrice-daily Post Office deliveries in the Clapham district, with two daily collections also. By now there were thirteen stagecoach services between Clapham and London. Around 1829, a special service for theatregoers left London at 12.15 a.m.

One of the group of North Side houses, known as Church Buildings, had been the home of abolitionist Granville Sharp. Later it became a boarding school for ex-slave children brought from Sierra Leone by Zachary Macaulay. This experiment was short-lived because of the unsuitability of the climate and the boys were returned to Sierra Leone. To compensate the head teacher, it became a school for the sons of leading families in the locality, among whom was future Whig politician Thomas Babbington Macaulay. Clapham Grammar School for Boys opened its doors in 1834. And it was from a boarding school for young ladies at Church House in Church Row that Percy Bysshe Shelley met Harriet Westbrook, with whom he eloped (but not from Clapham) in 1811.

The urbanisation of Clapham led to the building of new churches. The original parish church, dating from the twelfth century, had fallen into a state of grievous disrepair and was finally demolished in 1815. It was also too small for its growing congregation and some distance away from the locality's new centre of large mansions around the Common itself. The trustees of the new venture were headed by the Speaker of the House of Commons and wealthy merchant banker, John

Thornton. The new Church of the Holy Trinity (the Church on the Common) was consecrated in 1776.

The first and absentee rector, the Revd Sir John Stonehouse Bt. DCL, Squire of Radley, died in 1792. John Thornton and his friends had been greatly affected by the preaching of John Wesley, and their evangelical enthusiasm found expression in their drawing rooms and company boardrooms. To ensure the appointment of the right man as the second rector, Thornton bought the right of the living. Under the terms of his will, John Venn was appointed rector of the parish where he had been born in 1759. During this incumbency the building was extended and improved, with its 1,400 seats were invariably full and a second beadle appointed to control the carriages of the congregation.

This was the period of the 'Clapham Sect', the name mockingly given to John Venn and his group of evangelical parishioners, among whom were Henry Thornton, John's son, who was MP for Clapham, Zachary Macaulay and William Wilberforce MP. The sect exerted great influence as they 'laboured for national righteousness, and the conversion of the heathen, and rested not until the curse of slavery was swept away from all parts of the British Dominions.'[2]

It is clear that there developed a happy relationship between the parish church and the Congregationalists during this period, a time when the theological ethos of the latter changed quite dramatically.

Other churches appeared, too. The first Baptist evangelist was John Dolman, a basket maker from Blackman Street, Southwark, who preached in a barn near the Plough Tavern. A Baptist meeting house was built on South Side in 1877, but it became too small and a second building was erected in Grafton Square in 1882. By the 1960s this had become the home of the 'People's Church'. A second Baptist cause was established on the Wandsworth Road in 1873.

Methodism appeared on Clapham High Street and claimed to serve people from less elevated social positions than either the

Church on the Common or the Congregationalists could. The first Roman Catholic services were conducted by Redemptorist Fathers in a local house, some years before St Mary's Church was consecrated by Cardinal Wiseman in 1851. The adjacent monastery opened in 1895 became the Redemptorist mother house for England and Wales. Here Madame Adelina Patti was married in 1868. The Elim Foursquare Gospel Alliance opened one of its earliest churches in Clapham in 1922 and four years later its Bible College came to a former Redemptoristine Convent in Clapham Park.

3

Gathering Together

THE EXACT DATE of the beginning of dissent in Clapham is not known. The London Metropolitan Archives website declares that 'the Independent Congregation at Clapham was founded in 1645'. Earlier records are not so definite on this matter. The Revd James Hill, in the opening address 'the Narration... read at the opening of the New Church, 29th Sept. 1852', stated that 'Between the years 1640 & 1650 there was an Independent or Congregational Church at Clapham gathered, as it is supposed, by the Rev. W. Bridge'. The church manual for 1900 repeats Hill's statement: 'There is reason to believe that a Congregational Church was formed at Clapham between 1640 and 1650...'

Under the heading, 'Historic Church's Triple Anniversary – Birth of Congregationalism in London Recalled – 280 Years Ago,' the local weekly newspaper, the *Clapham Observer* of 25 September 1925, contained an extensive report of a meeting at the church on the previous evening. The report opened with the following paragraph:

> Clapham Congregational Church, Grafton Square – the fourth oldest [this is incorrect, by the way] of its denomination in the country – is this week celebrating the 280th of its foundation; the 73rd anniversary of the erection of the present building, and the tenth anniversary of the present minister, the Rev. G. Stanley Russell.

The same newspaper on 26 September 1930, again in a long article, says that, 'The foundation of the church dates back with reasonable certainty to 1645. Records with regard *H.C.F. News* [Home Churches Fund] to the history of the earliest years are unfortunately lacking.'

Then, the London Congregational Union in May 1956 published in its *H.C.F. News*, special bulletin No. 3:

> There are not many Congregational Churches in London which can trace their history back to the period before the Declaration of Indulgence of Charles II in 1672. One such Church was established as early as 1645, if not, indeed, earlier, in Clapham.

However, every reference to the foundation of the church during the ministry of the author (1967–73) said 'founded in 1645, if not 1640'. Some of the claims noted above are clearly inaccurate. As we have seen, London's first congregation, founded at Southwark in 1616 by Henry Jacob, was preceded by Gainsborough, Scrooby and Worksop, all in 1606. Welsh dissent began at Llanfaches in 1639, followed by Mynyddbach, Swansea, around 1640, with episodes in Cardiff and Wrexham, around 1640/1641. The Bishop of Exeter stated that there were eleven Separatist congregations in London around this period. This collection of dates highlights the lack of precision in dating events during the seventeenth century, particularly with regard to the founding of Dissenting congregations. What is more certain is the names of the men involved in the beginnings of Dissent in Clapham.

The first clear evidence of a conventicle in Clapham appears in the record of licences issued under the Declaration of Indulgence of 1672 but, as has been noted, there is a strong tradition which says the church originated in 1645, if not 1640.[1] According to Anthony à Wood's *Athenae Oxonienses*[2] there is a strong probability that Congregationalism took root here at around that time and that it is linked with three names: John Arthur, Jeremiah Burroughs (or Burroughes) and William Bridge. All three men entered Emmanuel College, Cambridge, during the reign of King James I, and it seems likely that they were contemporaries at the college.

It is thought that John Arthur was born sometime before 1600, the son of Laurence Arthur of Springfield, Essex, and was thus older than the other two men. He married Anne, the daughter of Miles Corbet, MP for Great Yarmouth.[3] They had one son, John. The living at Clapham fell vacant in 1642 and, because the patron Richard Atkins was a minor, the king presented the living to John Arthur, who was instituted as rector of Clapham on 22 May 1642. A man of moderate views, he established a Congregational church within the parish, its members attending Sunday worship at the parish church but also meeting for separate worship, prayer and Bible study at other times. This is the so-called 'New England pattern' and distinct from that of Separatism.

The parish prospered spiritually under his guidance and looked outward, as is testified to by a collection of £46 to aid the propagation of the Gospel among the Indians of North America. It was thought that John Arthur was ejected in 1662 'but he seems to have retained living there until he died'.[4] He was buried in Clapham on 27 March 1663, with his successor being instituted on 18 August 1663. In 1661 Arthur had been too infirm to receive his DD in person and this may possibly be the reason for him being allowed to remain as a resident of the parish. According to E. E. Cleal in *The Story of Congregationalism in Surrey*, Arthur was 'one spoken of by Calamy as a very considerable man and a moderate Nonconformist'.[5]

Meanwhile, Bridge and Burroughs had been active in East Anglia. It had become the practice for those who were dissatisfied with the ministry of the incumbent to raise money to pay a lecturer to preach at the parish church at a time other than that of the ordinary service.

Jeremiah Burroughs was born in London in 1599. He was admitted to Emmanuel College, Cambridge, as a 'pensioner' (scholar) in 1617, graduating with a BA in 1621 and MA in

1624. His Puritanism caused him to leave Cambridge. He was an assistant to Edmund Calamy in Bury St Edmunds before becoming rector of Tivetshall, Norfolk, in 1631.

In 1635 Matthew Wren[6] became Bishop of Norwich; he was a strong supporter of the archbishop of Canterbury, Thomas Laud. Wren pursued a vigorous campaign against Puritans, with separate articles of inquiry forming the basis of visits to his parishes. Church wardens and others were required to take an oath 'that shall be sworn to make presentments' under nine headings 'concerning religion and doctrine', worship at their church, its 'furniture and possessions; matrimony; the Church Wardens and Side-men; the parishioners; Ministers, Preachers and Lecturers; Schoole-masters, Physicians, Chyrugions [Surgeons], Midwives and Parish-Clarkes; and Ecclesiastical Officers.'[7] Wren also set about enforcing the reading of the *Declaration of Sports*.

Also known as the *Book of Sports*, the *Declaration* was issued by James I in 1617 to resolve a dispute between Lancashire Puritans and the local gentry, many of whom were Roman Catholic. It listed the games and recreations that were permitted on Sundays and other Holy days, and a year later, in 1618, it was applied to the whole of England (and Wales). The sports allowed included archery, dancing, 'leaping, vaulting or other such harmless recreation', together with 'May-games, Whitsun-ales, Morris-dancers and the setting up of May Poles'. Puritans and other 'precise people' were rebuked for their demand for strict abstinence on the Christian Sabbath, while Roman Catholics and others were condemned for not attending their parish churches. Only those who had first attended their parish church were allowed to participate in these pastimes.

Charles I re-issued the *Declaration* on 18 October 1633 as 'The King's Majesty's declaration to his subjects concerning lawful sports to be used'. All ministers were commanded to read it to their congregations at Sunday worship. Those who refused were to be deprived of their livings. Puritan hostility to the *Book of Sports* grew alongside Puritan strength in Parliament. Enforcement of the order ended with the fall of Archbishop Thomas Laud in 1640 and the *Book of Sports* was burned publicly by order of Parliament in 1643, two years before Laud's execution.

Burroughs refused to obey both bishop and king, and was suspended in 1636 and deprived of his living in 1637. For some months he joined the household of the Earl of Warwick, possibly as domestic chaplain but again he was deprived – this time on a charge of seditious speeches during the Scottish wars. Several friendly patrons offered him a living, but he chose to go with William Bridge to Rotterdam, the Netherlands, in 1637. In Rotterdam the two Puritans joined the Independent Church founded by Hugh Peters in 1631, and this church gave them a warm welcome. Within months of his arrival, Burroughs was chosen a preacher/teacher by the church, and Bridge was elected as pastor.

By late autumn 1640 it was safe for the exiles to return to England, which they did the following year. Burroughs was appointed morning (7 a.m.) lecturer at Stepney on 6 September 1641, together with William Greenwood. Burroughs became known as 'the morning star of Stepney'[8]. He was invited to preach before the House of Commons and House of Lords on several occasions. His fellow Dissenter, Thomas Brooks, described him as 'a prince of preachers'.

Burroughs was a delegate to the Westminster Assembly of Divines (1643–9), which was appointed by the Long Parliament to restructure the Church of England. During these years the Assembly produced documents which constituted the major confessional standards of the Presbyterian faith, including the Westminster Confession of Faith, the Westminster Larger Catechism, the Westminster Shorter Catechism, and the Directory of Public Worship. The Assembly was overwhelmingly Presbyterian in make-up, though it did include an Erastian group favouring the state's control over ecclesiastical law. Burroughs was joined at the Assembly by his two fellow-exiles in Rotterdam, William Bridge and Sidrach Simpson, who, with Philip Nye and Thomas Goodwin formed the Five Dissenting Brethren, strenuously opposing Presbyterian intolerance in the interest of Independency.

Throughout his ministry Burroughs remained a moderate, in keeping with the motto on his study door in Greek and Latin: *Opinionum varietas et opiniantium unitas non sunt hasustata* (Difference of belief and unity of believers are not inconsistent). The Puritan leader and poet Richard Baxter commented 'If all the Episcopalians had been like Archbishop Ussher, all the Presbyterians like Stephen Marshall, and all the Independents like Jeremiah Burroughs, the breaches of the Church would soon have been healed.'

William Bridge was born in Cambridgeshire in 1600, a year after Burroughs. He was a student at Emmanuel College, Cambridge, receiving his MA in 1626 and being elected a Fellow. Bridge was elected to a lectureship in Colchester in 1631. From 1633 to 1636 he was supported as Friday preacher at St George's Church in Tombland by Norwich Corporation. From 1637 he was rector of St Peter Hungate, Norwich, and St George, Tombland.

As noted, on his appointment as archbishop of Canterbury, Thomas Laud had ordered his bishops to report on the state of religion in their dioceses. Richard Corbet, bishop of Norwich, informed the archbishop that he had suppressed several lectureships; among the clergy named was Bridge, curate of St George's, and he was suspended until he submitted to Episcopal authority. As has been noted, the Laudian bishop Matthew Wren was appointed to Norwich in 1635. Article thirteen of his impeachment by the Long Parliament states that Bridge and Burroughs, with 50 others:

> ... were excommunicated, suspended or deprived, and otherwise censured and silenced, to the undoing of the wives and children... for not reading the second service at the communion table set altarwise, for not reading the *Book of Sports*, for using conceived

prayers before and after sermons, and for not observing some
other illegal innovations by himself and his under officers.

Norwich diocesan records show that Bridge did not obey
a summons to appear before the Consistory Court in 1636
when the bishop silenced, deprived and excommunicated
him. Wren reported to Laud on 7 December 1636 that, 'Mr
Bridge hath left two cures and is removed into Holland.' Laud
passed this information to the king, who wrote in his own
hand in the margin of the report, 'Let him go, we are well be
rid of him.'

In Rotterdam, Bridge renounced his Anglican ordination,
becoming an ordinary member of the congregation until,
as we have seen, he was appointed pastor of the church in
1638, being inducted by John Ward. In the following year he
was received into Leiden University's *honoris gratia* and was
succeeded as pastor by Sidrach Simpson.

On returning to England in 1641 Bridge sprung into
activity. He preached a sermon entitled, 'Babylon's Downfall',
'before sundry of the Honourable House of Commons at
Westminster'.[9] He also received an invitation to visit Yarmouth
as a preacher, and eventually settled there in 1642. He had
gathered a Congregational church in Norwich that year too
and this moved to Yarmouth in 1643. In the same year he
preached before King Charles I, making a direct attack on
the queen. During the meetings of the Westminster Assembly,
whereas Burroughs was able to fulfil his ministry at Stepney,
Bridge was too far away from Yarmouth, but he was still able
to preach at various London churches. After his ejection from
Yarmouth he preached sometimes in Clapham.

Anthony à Wood reports that Bridge was:

> ... a frequent preacher before the Long Parliament, a notorious
> independent, and a keeper up of that faction by continual
> preaching during the time of the usurpation, silenced upon his
> Majesty's return, carried on his cause with the said Jeremiah

31

Burroughes in conventicles at Clapham in Surrey till about the time of his death, which happened in 1670.

William Bridge died in Yarmouth on 12 March 1670 aged 70. According to historian Daniel Neal, 'he was a good scholar and had a well stocked library; a hard student, who rose every morning, winter and summer, at four o'clock; he was an excellent preacher, a candid and very charitable man, who did much good by his ministry.'[10]

4

Scattered!

THE RESTORATION OF the monarchy in 1660 brought troubled times to Clapham's rector and his flock. As noted, John Arthur was ejected from his living in 1662, though it appears that he was allowed to live in the locality because of ill health. His successor in Clapham was John Gurgany DD, a canon at Salisbury cathedral. The new rector was also a sick man. The parish records for 1670 show 'that he was so infirm that at a meeting of the parishioners it was resolved to pay twenty shillings to each minister that preached that Sabbath day.' And *Calamy Revised* notes, 'It is not improbable that the Puritan antecedents of the parish, combined with the feebleness of the incumbent, may have secured for the Nonconformists of Clapham a certain degree of toleration or at least prevented them from being rigorously hunted down.'[1]

However, all was not at a loss for the Clapham Dissenters, for now they were joined by no less than seven leading men in the Puritan cause who'd been ejected from elsewhere. Of the seven, three were granted licences as 'Presbyterian preachers' under the Declaration of Indulgence of 1672, when their houses were also licensed as Nonconformist meeting places. They were Thomas Lye, Dr Henry Wilkinson, and William Hughes.

Thomas Lye (or Lee or Leigh) applied for a licence for himself and his house on 11 April 1672. His application was at first refused, but eventually granted the fourth time on 30 April. Lye was born in Chard, Somerset, on 25 March 1621. He became a student at Wadham College, Oxford, in 1636 and a scholar from the following year, graduating with a BA in 1641. When Charles I assembled his army in Oxford at the beginning of the Civil War in 1642, Lye moved to Emmanuel College, Cambridge, where he took his MA in 1646. For a short time he was headmaster of Bury St Edmunds School. When the parliamentary army occupied Oxford, Lye returned to be chaplain of Wadham College, receiving his Oxford MA in 1649.

Soon afterwards he returned to Chard. New troubles began in August 1651 when he refused to sign the Covenant and was ordered to leave and remain at least ten miles from it; nor was he allowed to preach in any market town in Somerset. This sentence was reversed by the Council at Whitehall on 18 November 1651. Then, in 1654, he was made an assistant to the Committee for the Approbation of Publique Preachers, more usually known as the Triers, whose task it was to decide on the suitability of applicants for livings. In 1657 Lye accepted an invitation from parishioners to become minister of All Hallows, Lombard Street, London, replacing a Mr Cardell who was ejected by commissioners that same year. Two years later, in 1659, he was made one of 'the approvers of ministers according to the Presbyterian way'. He was a preacher at Dyers Hall, Thomas Street, London, from 1675.

It had become increasingly likely during 1659 that the monarchy would be restored and that Dissenters would face royalist revenge. However, they were relieved to hear the words of Charles I's son and heir, in his Declaration of Breda, read to the Convention Parliament on 1 May 1660, when he promised 'a liberty to tender consciences, and that no man be disquieted and called into question for differences of opinion in matters of religion.' At the same time, Charles II granted a free and general pardon to all his subjects, 'excepting only such persons as shall be exempted by Parliament' (i.e. the regicides). This became law in the Act of Free and General Pardon, Indemnity and Oblivion, which received royal assent on 21 August 1660.

As many Dissenters had been involved in the bitter struggles of the previous twelve years, they still had cause to fear an uncertain future. Nonetheless, at the restoration of the monarchy, Lye joined other ministers in expressing thanks to the king for 'his gracious concessions regarding ecclesiastical affairs.' Their gesture was in vain.

Within two years, a series of acts was passed, known collectively as the Clarendon Code. The chief of these was the Act of Uniformity, which became law on 19 May 1662, the preamble of which expressed abhorrence of the confusion introduced into English religion by the Dissenters. Under this act, the Book of Common Prayer of 1662 was the sole form of worship allowed within 'this realm of England, dominion of Wales, and town of Berwick-upon-Tweed.'[2] Every minister was expected to make a declaration of agreement within three months and, if necessary, seek episcopal ordination. Failure to do so would result in his being 'utterly disabled and all his ecclesiastical Promotions shall be void, as if he was naturally dead.' Clearly, the Declaration of Breda meant nothing.

The earlier Corporation Act of May 1661 ordered that all persons appointed to public office must receive 'the sacrament of the Lord's Supper according to the rites of the Church of England' within twelve months of his appointment. The Conventicle Act of 1664 banned the coming together of more than five adults for nonconformist worship. The last statute in what became known as the Clarendon Code was the Five Mile Act of 30 October 1665, which banned anyone caught preaching in an unlawful conventicle of coming within any city, town or borough which elected a Member of Parliament. A second Conventicle Act was passed in 1673 which, although its penalties were less severe, broadened the terms of reference of the first act, enabling the harrying of all who disobeyed. In the same year, the Test Act, primarily aimed at Roman Catholics, made life more difficult for all who failed to attend their parish church and receive Communion.

An informer stated in 1665 that Lye 'had been lately in Scotland and was now teaching school at Clapham, Surrey, and preaching at Morgan's Lane, Southwark'. The Episcopal

Returns for 1669, in listing the conventicles in the deanery of Southwark, make reference to one meeting 'in Morgan's Lane, att the house of one Cholmeley, a brewer, who hath bin detected with false tunes to cheat the excise.' The congregation is described as 'of pretty good Qualitie', led by 'Mr Lye, a Nonconformist minister.' Anthony à Wood in *Athenae Oxonienses* adds:

> I know not... anything else of him only he dying ar Bednal Green near London on 7th day of June in 1684, was buried in the Church at Clapham in Surrey, in which town he usually held forth in conventicles with Dr Hen. Wilkinson, commonly called Long Harry, and Will. Bridge, sometime minister of Yarmouth. He also for a better livelihood instructed the sons of Nonconformists.

Calamy Revised continues:

> In a lawsuit, Attorney General v Hewer 1700, some particulars of him were given by one of his old scholars at Clapham, that he went to the parish church but preached in his own house after church-time; that for his Nonconformity he was imprisoned in the Marshallsea, after which he ceased teaching school publicly; used to come to town on Saturday nights to preach at a conventicle on Sundays; taught Catechism on Saturday afternoons at Dyers Hall... He was presented at the General Sessions, Guildhall, 16 April 1683, as holding conventicles.

Edmund Calamy, author of *The Nonconformist's Memorial* (1702), recalled being taken by his mother 'to good old Mr Lye... she being catechised of him in her younger days', adding that Lye had 'a most tender affection for the young'. Calamy was one of his scholars at the age of fourteen. Lye's published works included sermons, *An Exposition of the Westminster Shorter Catechism* (1676) and a book entitled *The Child's Delight* (1671), containing an English grammar and spelling book intermixed with moral principles. He was a signatory to *An Epistle commending Thomas Vincent's Exposition of the Westminster Shorter Catechism* and the 1623 Puritan *Preface to the Scottish Metrical Psalter.* Other published works included two 'Farewell Sermons', a sermon entitled 'Death, the Sweetest Sleep' and several of the 'Cripplegate Sermons'. After the death of his first wife, Rebecca, he married Sarah (who died in 1678). Of his large family only two daughters survived him. Thomas Lye died in Bethnal Green on 7 June 1684, and was buried in Clapham four days later.

Henry Wilkinson – one of two ejected clergy bearing that name – was the second applicant requesting to register his house as a Nonconformist meeting place. He was born on 4 March 1610, at Waddensden, Buckinghamshire, where his father, another Henry, a Fellow of Merton College, served as rector of the parish from 1601, and was chosen as one of the Westminster Divines in 1643. He died in 1647.

Henry Wilkinson entered Magdalen College, Oxford, at the age of twelve and was awarded his BA in 1626, an MA in 1629 and a BD in 1638. He was ordained and became a lecturer at his old university. He preached regularly in the Oxford area, not without 'girds against the actions and certain men of the time'.[3] In 1640 he was suspended from preaching and divine lecturing by the vice-chancellor at Magdalen Hall 'until he should recant' because of an outspoken sermon on 'lukewarmness,' containing an attack also on empty ritual, which he preached at the university church of St Mary's on 6 September. He appealed to the Long Parliament and was restored by the Committee on Religion on 23 December 1640. The committee also ordered that his sermon be printed. When King Charles I moved to Oxford, Wilkinson fled to London in 1643, becoming rector of St Faith's under St Paul's, Castle Baynard Ward, in August 1644 and was chosen a member of the Westminster Assembly. In 1645 he was appointed rector of St Dunstan in the East.

After King Charles I had been driven from Oxford, Wilkinson was one of the six preachers sent to the city by Parliament in 1646. He was elected Senior Fellow of Magdalen College, Oxford, a position he held for the next sixteen years, as well as being deputed as a parliamentary visitor to Oxford University. Two years later he was appointed Canon of Christ Church College, Oxford, by Parliament and was awarded an Oxford doctorate in Divinity in 1649. Then, in 1652, he became Lady Margaret Professor of Divinity, holding the chair until his ejectment in 1660. In 1654 he served on the commission for ejecting scandalous ministers in Oxfordshire. He was commonly known as Long Harry, to distinguish him from his college's 'Dean Harry', another Puritan divine with the same name.

After the Restoration in 1660, he moved first to All Hallows, Lombard Street, London. During this period, a conventicle of some 60 or more persons to whom he was preaching was broken up in Camberwell in August 1665, and some of the congregation were arrested.[4] Wilkinson moved to Clapham, where he opened a school and, after the 1672 Declaration of Indulgence, he was licensed as a Presbyterian to preach at both his house and school-house. He married Lady Vere, née Carr, a member of the Stanley family and had one son and two daughters. Wilkinson died on 5 June 1675. Many hundreds attended his funeral service at Drapers' Hill and he was buried at St Dunstan's. He was described by Anthony à Wood as 'a good scholar, a close student and an excellent preacher,' though describing his voice as 'shrill in speaking and whining, and that his sermons were full of confusion'. Wood also recorded that when the stained glass was taken from Christ Church cathedral, Oxford, Wilkinson 'furiously stampt upon many parts'.

The recipient of the third licence was one William Hughes, whose house was also licensed as a meeting place. It is believed that this was the son of William and Parnell Hughes of Bedminster and he was baptised in Bromham on 17 July 1619. He entered New Inn Hall, Oxford, gaining his BA in 1638 and an MA in 1641. Ordained in Salisbury on 22 December 1639, he was appointed the curate of Bromham. It was during this time that he met his wife, Judith Lea. They were married in Bromham in 1642 and had six children. He served as vicar of St Mary's, Marlborough (1649–62) and also as minister and lecturer at St Peter's church, Marlborough, from 1649. In 1654 he was appointed an assistant to the Wiltshire Commission. After his ejection from his parish home, Hughes bought a house in Marlborough where he taught 'a large school' and 'several gentlemen of the county sent their children to him,' as also did several in London.[5] He was licensed as a Congregationalist to preach at his house in Marlborough and gathered a church around himself and remained in the town until his death on 14 February 1687. 'His life after ejection was one continu'd Scene of Trouble.' He was the subject of several Bishop's Court citations. 'For several years, as it were, a prisoner in his own house, not daring to be known to be at home with his family, for fear of being carried away by force.'[6] It may well be that he was forced to leave Marlborough for a while and came to Clapham in 1670. He was buried at St Mary's church in Marlborough.

Three other Nonconformists of note were recorded as having preached in Clapham. Onesiphorus Rood, born, possibly, in 1621, was the son of Edward Rood of Thame, Oxfordshire. He entered New Inn Hall, Oxford, gaining his BA in 1641. He then proceeded to Emmanuel College, Cambridge, receiving his MA in 1645. He was curate of Tothill Fields Church from 1648 until his ejection, and Parliament appointed him chaplain to the House of Lords after the expulsion of the bishops. At this time he lived in Hackney where, in September and October 1682, 'Onesiphorus Roode, clerk,' was brought before Sir Clement Armiger JP at the Middlesex Sessions, charged with having twice 'preached to and taught the persons assembled at two unlawful conventicles, held under colour of exercising religion at the dwelling-house in the said parish of George Hockenhull esq. of Hackney.'[7] The preacher was fined £20 for the first offence and £40 for the second. Later he moved to Clapham, where he preached frequently during the reign of William III. On leaving Clapham he lived privately until his death at 'upwards of ninety years of age'[8].

Richard Jennings was born in Ipswich, the son of another Richard Jennings, by his first wife Elizabeth, who was the daughter of Edmund Daye MP. He was baptised in St Lawrence's Church, Ipswich, on 4 August 1616. He entered St Catherine's College, Cambridge, and was awarded his BA in 1637 and MA in 1642. Jennings underwent a conversion when walking in his father's garden in April 1636. Two years later on 1 June 1638 he sailed to Massachusetts Bay with Nathaniel Rogers and other Puritans, arriving five months later on 16 November. By the time he left the Rogers family after Christmas his stormy voyage of conversion was complete. His return to England, which commenced in December 1638, was also eventful. His ship ran onto the rocks in the bay of St Michael's Mount, Cornwall.

He then became chaplain to Mrs Elms Warmington in Northamptonshire. Later he was appointed curate in North Glenham, Suffolk, and was ordained in London on 18 September 1645. In September 1647 he became rector of Grundisburgh, Suffolk, before proceeding to a similar appointment in Coombs in the same county in 1647. He was twice married: first to Temperance, daughter of the owner of Coombs Hall, who bore him three sons and two daughters and, after her death, to Susan, daughter of Robert Reeve of Thwaite. Though ejected in 1662, he was allowed to remain at the parsonage until 1678. Nonetheless, his ejectment under the Act of Uniformity caused him great financial problems:

> I was in debt one hundred and sixty pounds, and had but little coming in for myself, wife and children, and was also some years after unjustly forced to discharge a bond of fifty pounds. And the educating and disposing of my three sisters stood me in two hundred pounds. Yet, by God's merciful providence, by degrees I discharged all my debts.[9]

On 10 June 1672 he was licensed as a Nonconformist preacher in Coombs. On leaving the parsonage he moved to

Clapham for the last three years of his life, becoming chaplain to Madam Gould. *Calamy Revised* states that he spent the 'latter part of his life with three pious widows at Clapham,' adding, 'A man of true piety and sound learning, he retain'd his juvenile learning and he was still able to preach without notes at the age of ninety-two.'

Jennings died 12 September 1709, and was buried in Clapham two days later. According to *Calamy Revised*, 'he passed through the world without noise and ostentation, and without ever appearing in print.' The Madam Gould named was the second wife of John Gould (1616–79), one of the agents for obtaining indulgences for nonconformists in 1672. Madam Judith Gould died in 1704, and was buried in Clapham on 24 July. Her home was a meeting place for Congregationalists in Clapham.

The last of the occasional preachers was John Hutchinson. Born in London in April 1638, he was educated at Merchant Taylors' School and Eton, before progressing to Cambridge, where he graduated with a BA in 1659. At the age of 24 he was elected a Fellow of Trinity College. He was ejected in 1662 for not conforming 'to the forms and ceremonies of the publick worship'.[10] Employment was offered by Joseph Hall to correct of Schrevelius' Lexicon, with Hall correcting the Greek-Latin and Hutchinson the Latin-Greek.

Then John Hutchinson travelled to France and Italy, where he studied physics and anatomy. On returning to England he was offered a Fellowship of the College of Physicians, but waived it. He was licensed to practise as a physician *per totam Angliam* and pursued his calling in Hitchin for some 30 years. He then moved to Clapham around 1700, where he 'practis'd Physick with a great deal of Reputation and Skill, preaching gratuitously there for some two years.' Six years later he moved to Hackney to run a boarding school and it was there that he died on 9 February 1713, predeceasing his wife Sophia by two and a half years.

5

Settled!

AFTER 1673 THE church in Clapham met at various private houses, and the home of a Madam Gould was often named. It was around this time, somewhere between 1673 and 1675, that the church called its first 'minister in the formal sense'.[1]

Philip Lamb was born in 1622, the son of Henry Lamb, minister of Cerne Abbas, Dorset. A graduate at Clare College, Cambridge, he was awarded his BA in 1646. From 1648 to 1655 he was rector of Alton Pancras, Dorset, leaving there to become rector of Bere Regis in the same county, but without episcopal ordination.

In 1662 he resigned as vicar of Bere Regis, rather than face the choice of accepting a bishop's hands upon his head or ejection.

> He can therefore be considered the founder of Bere Regis Congregational Church... In his farewell sermon he said, 'I may not speak from God to you, yet I shall not cease to speak to God for you...' Later he was forced to flee to Morden... Later still he moved to Alton Pancras near Cerne Abbas. On 1 May 1672 he was granted a licence to be a 'Congregational Teacher' at his house in East Morden. Later still a convenient meeting house in Winterborne Kingston, probably the residence of Richard Woolfreys was provided for him, where the people flocked from all parts to hear him. His licence was recalled 'when great severity was us'd'. Persecution drove him to flee to Clapham, London, where the church met at the home of Madam Gould.[2]

Calamy Revised speaks of 'a great general lamentation

when he was silenced'. His many predecessors, including Bridge and Burroughes, Wilkinson, Lye and Hughes, had been occasional preachers rather than pastors of the flock. Thus Lamb may be regarded as the first full-time minister of Clapham Congregational church. He died in Clapham on 25 March 1689, in his 67th year, and was buried there three days later. His wife Elizabeth lived for another twelve years. They had four sons and three daughters.

Calamy Revised comments that 'he was offered six hundred a year if he would have conformed, but it did not tempt him. He was remarkable for his unaffected piety, cheerful temperament, and engaging disposition...' John Waddington's *Surrey Congregational History* (1866), states that Lamb preached the funeral services of John Gould, possibly the husband of Madam Gould, at whose house the church had met, and Mrs Mary Lye. The latter could either be a mistake for Mrs Sarah Lye, wife of Thomas Lye, or some other relative of his.

6

Growing Church

EDWARD GRACE WAS Philip Lamb's successor as minister of Clapham church, serving there from 1689 until his death in 1714. Grace was elected a manager of the Congregational Fund in 1696. The only surviving record of his work consists of two sermons preached by him at the Clapham funerals of Mr and Mrs Crisp, copies of which are kept at the British Museum. Mr Crisp was one of the oldest members of the church.

From 1697 to 1706 Edward Grace was assisted at the afternoon service by Edmund Batson. Batson, who was educated at Taunton Academy, began to preach in 1693. From 1694 to 1697 he ministered at Ilminster. He came to Clapham in 1697 where he remained until 1706. As his Clapham duties were limited to afternoon services, he assisted a Mr Sheffield at St Thomas' (Southwark) in the morning. Edmund Batson then moved to Taunton, where he succeeded his former teacher, Matthew Warren, and Emmanuel Hartford as pastor of the church known as Paul's Meeting. In 1730 a Mr Amory was appointed to assist him there.

Although requiring his on account of his advanced age and many infirmities as of the great labours of his office, he would not relinquish any part of his salary, which so displeased some members of his congregation, that they withdrew and formed another society of which Mr Amory became the pastor. Before the division, the Presbyterian congregation at Taunton consisted of fifteen hundred hearers, and so great was the throng, that unless persons went early it was with difficulty that they got to their pews.

Mr Batson was entirely laid aside by the infirmities of age for two years before his death, which happened in 1735.[1]

In Clapham Batson was followed by Moses Lowman, who acted as assistant to Grace from 1710 until 1714. Lowman was ordained and became sole pastor, a role he held until his death in 1752, and his ministry of 38 years was the longest in the church's history, exceeding that of Dr Guinness Rogers by three years.

Moses Lowman had been born in London in 1680. His father had been 'intended for the Church' and was educated in Cambridge, but he chose instead a secular career, possibly because of his Nonconformity. He intended that his son should take up law and, accordingly, Moses entered the Middle Temple in 1697. His time there was short indeed, for on 17 September 1698 he went to the Netherlands and enrolled at the University of Leiden. There, and in Utrecht, he studied under two leading theologians, Dr De Vries and Hermann Witsius, who provided him with the foundations on which he developed his noted scholarship, especially his proficiency in Hebraic studies.

The period of Lowman's ministry in Clapham coincided with a decline in religious enthusiasm in England, caused by growing scepticism and rationalism, and the growth in individualism and utilitarianism. Nonetheless, persecution was far from dead. 'A Parliamentary return of 1715 puts the damage done to Nonconformist chapels in Surrey at £5,268-12-7½ and, though there is no direct evidence, there is a tradition that this church at Clapham suffered.'[2]

Lowman's gift lay in writing rather than preaching. Bogue and Bennett in *History of Dissenters* say this of him in 1810 during the Evangelical Revival:

> While Mr Lowman claims a high degree of commendation as a writer, there is none due to him as a preacher. An intelligent man, who was his constant hearer, declared that he could never understand him. In the few sermons which he published there

is something remarkably awkward, rugged and clumsy, and very little calculated to attract the attention of an audience. It is painful to be obliged to find fault with a man who is an able writer, because he is a bad preacher, but for such a fault severe reprehension is due.

Lowman's *Dissertation on the Civil Government of the Hebrews* was written in response to Tory slanders on the Jews, while his *Seven Periods of the Apocalypse* greatly influenced Jonathan Edwards in his interpretation of the Book of Revelation. The British Museum lists eighteen entries of works by Lowman in its possession.

When the ministers of the three denominations met together at The George tavern in London on 11 July 1727 to decide how to resist attacks on the Toleration Act, Lowman was one of the six Congregational ministers present.

Moses Lowman died on 3 May 1752 and on Sunday, 14 June, the Revd Samuel Chandler preached the following sermon at the Clapham church, 'The Character and Reward of a Christian Bishop – a Sermon occasioned by the lamented death of the late Reverend Mr Moses Lowman, who departed this life, May 3, 1752, aged 72.'

Dr Philip Furneaux followed Moses Lowman. Furneaux was born in Totnes in December 1726 and came to London around 1742 to study for the ministry under Dr Jennings at the Academy in Wellhouse Street. Jennings, a convinced Calvinist, was dismayed to note that many of his students 'became tinged with the prevalent Arianism of the day',[3] and expelled several of them for heresy. Despite being one such tainted student, Furneaux – who remained at the Academy until 1749, probably assisting Jennings in the last few years – was ordained in 1749 and assisted Henry Read at St Thomas' Presbyterian Church, Southwark, until 1753, when he received an invitation to Clapham. Meanwhile, in 1752, he had become one of the two evening lecturers at Salter's Hall, Cannon Street. In 1767 he was awarded the degree of DD by Marischal College, Aberdeen.

Writing in the *Protestant Dissenters' Magazine* in 1798, Joshua
Toulmin says:

> For many years Dr Furneaux had an alternate with Dr Prior in the
> lecture on the Lord's Day evening at Salter's Hall, where he always
> preached to a full and attentive auditory, to whom the good sense,
> a scriptural strain, and an easy flow of language recommended his
> discourses, which were delivered, though not entirely according
> to the proprieties of elocution, with a natural fervour which
> commanded the ear and heart.

Bogue and Bennett were not so generous in their comments:
'His composition was truly elegant, but his delivery, by poring
over his notes, and a whine which would have disgraced a
Scotch seceder, was most disagreeable.'

However, Furneaux's defects were more than matched
by his great ability and force of personality. The Clapham
congregation flourished under his ministry, so that it needed a
large new meeting house, which was erected in Clapham Old
Town in 1762.

Furneaux's leadership extended far beyond his
congregation. He became a Coward's trustee[4] and took up a
similar role with Dr Williams' Foundations[5] between 1766
and 1778. Above all else, he became passionate in his struggle
for religious liberty.

It had been the practice of the City of London to allow those
persons elected as sheriff to decline their appointment on
payment of a fine of £400. In 1730 the City decided to place such
fines in a fund to pay for a new Mansion House. As Dissenters
were barred from public office by the Test and Corporation
Act, they became an easy target for the City Corporation. On
30 April 1751, Allen Evans, a Baptist deacon was nominated.
Evans wrote to the Lord Mayor on 14 May to explain why, as a
Dissenter, he was unable to accept.

The City decided to take action against him and two other
Dissenters, George Streatfield and Alexander Sheaff, for
refusing to pay the fine. The case against Streatfield had to be

dropped, but the other two were brought before the Sheriff's Court and the Court of Hustings under a recent bye-law dealing with this offence. Both courts found them guilty but the two men, with the backing of Dissenting Deputies, appealed to the now defunct Court of St Martin's, where the judges found in their favour. The Corporation's appeal to the House of Lords on 21 January 1767 was lost, with six of the seven judges siding with the defendants. The Lord Chief Justice, Lord Mansfield, stated that anyone who had not received Communion in the Church of England within the previous year could not be appointed to such offices. He added that a Dissenter was not a criminal because he declined Anglican Communion – he was specifically released from that obligation by the Toleration Act of 1769.

Lord Mansfield's judgment against the Corporation was celebrated by Dissenters as a great victory. The judgment was remembered verbatim by Philip Furneaux, 'who richly deserved the pipe of wine with which the Deputies presented him for his remarkable feat of reproducing this long judgement from memory.'[6]

In 1769, the fourth volume of Mr Justice William Blackstone's *Commentaries on the Laws of England* was published, in which the author affirmed that, in the eyes of the law, Nonconformity was a crime. In the following year Furneaux refuted this argument in his *Letters to the Honourable Mr Justice Blackstone* (1770). There followed a debate in writing between the two men which gained much attention. In addition to that work, Furneaux published five or six sermons and *Essay on Toleration* (1773). The Clapham minister played a leading part in the seven-year war of pamphlets which culminated in the passing of an act in 1779 which enabled Nonconformists to make a declaration of Protestant belief instead of subscribing to the 39 Articles of the Church of England.

Furneaux, however, was completely unaware of his victory, for in 1777 he was struck down by hereditary insanity, which must have been accentuated by overtaxing himself. He died at a private asylum on 23 November 1783. A public subscription for his maintenance raised £10,000 and Lord Mansfield was among the subscribers.

At the beginning of the twentieth century the Charity Commission drew up a scheme, which supported not Furneaux's church in Clapham but two Unitarian institutions, the Ministers' Benefit Society and Manchester College, Oxford. Like Lowman before him and Thomas Urwick after him, Furneaux deviated from orthodox Calvinism and was accused of Arianism (the denial of the divinity of Christ). Arianism was used as a term of abuse at the time by those who were alarmed by the emergence of Unitarianism and it was probably applied to Furneaux because of his demand for state toleration for religious dissent with the respecting of individual conscience and belief.

Furneaux became influential in American colonies which were increasingly concerned with the question of freedom. His *Letters on Toleration* (1770) were widely circulated in the colonies and Letter III appeared in an appendix to Sir William Blackstone's *Commentaries on the Laws of England*, a second edition of which was reprinted in Philadelphia in 1773. According to Theodore Albert Schroeder (1864–1953), the views and words of Philip Furneaux in that letter are so remarkably similar to those in the Virginia Religious Liberty Statute, drawn up later by Thomas Jefferson, that there is little doubt that Jefferson drew directly from Furneaux's letter. Jefferson is reputed to have declared that 'there is not an original thought or word in the "Virginia Religious Liberty Statute".' The *Letters on Toleration* still have an important place in American legal writings concerned with freedom and especially freedom of religion.[7]

When the demands of Clapham and Salter's Hall had become too much for Furneaux in 1777, a series of assistants was appointed to take Sunday afternoon service at Salter's Hall. The first assistant was Caleb Evans DD (1737–91) who was born in Bristol, the son of Baptist minister, Hugh Evans MA.

Caleb Evans received a grammar school education there before moving to London in 1753, where he was baptised at Little Wild Street Baptist Church by Dr Samuel Stennet. Evans became a student at Mile End Academy before becoming an assistant to the Revd Josiah Thompson at Unicorn Baptist Church, Southwark. In 1757 he was appointed to a similar role to assist Philip Furneaux in Clapham. But two years later he accepted his father's invitation to return to Bristol to assist him at Broadmead Baptist Church and its academy.

After the death of his father in 1781, Caleb Evans succeeded him and ministered there for 32 years in total. In 1770 he founded the charity Bristol Education Society in honour of his father. In 1789 he received the degree of DD from Aberdeen University. Caleb Evans advocated Open Communion among his fellow Baptists. He is chiefly remembered for his controversy with John Wesley on the subject of civil and religious liberty at the start of the American War of Independence. He died in 1791, in his 54th year.

Caleb Evans was followed in Clapham by Rice Harris DD. Harris was born in Wales in 1731 and entered the Mile End Academy around 1754, where he remained for three years until he was 'dismissed', presumably for theological reasons. He transferred to the Wellclose Square Academy of Dr Richard Jennings. Harris served as assistant in Clapham from 1762 to 1766, before taking up a similar post with Dr Jabez Earl in Hanover Street, Long Acre. Harris was ordained on 28 May 1768, becoming pastor at Hanover Street where he remained until his death on 10 October 1795. James Manning gave a sermon at Hanover Street on 25 October 1795 based on the life of Rice Harris.

The last assistant to be named at the Clapham church in this period was an orthodox Presbyterian, Samuel Morton Savage DD. Savage was born in London on 19 July 1721, the grandson of John Savage, pastor of the Seventh Day Baptist Church,

Mill Yard, Goodman's Fields. He claimed to be a descendent and the male heir of the second Earl Rivers. He was related to Hugh Boulton, archbishop of Armagh, an many assumed that he would seek holy orders, but that was not to be.

Having left grammar school in 1738, he was apprenticed to his uncle, Abraham Toulmin, an apothecary, who kept a school at Old Gravel Lane, Wapping. However Savage came under the influence of Isaac Watts and abandoned medicine for the ministry and trained at the Coward Fund Academy (where Philip Furneaux himself had been a student). Savage became an assistant tutor there in the Classics and natural sciences in 1742. He worked at home in Wellclose Square from 1744 until 1762, but then the academy transferred to Hoxton, where he taught divinity until the closure of the academy in 1785.

He gained the BD from King's College, Aberdeen, in 1764, and was awarded his DD by Marischal College, Aberdeen, in 1767. Alongside his academic work, Savage ministered for 40 years at the prestigious Duke's Place, Bury Street Congregational Church (formerly Mark Lane), St Mary Axe, where Isaac Watts had been minister. He was appointed assistant pastor in 1747, and after being ordained he became co-pastor in 1753. He served as sole pastor from 1757 until his resignation in 1787.

The length of his ministry there conceals the fact that he was not popular, owing to him being a bookish man who hid himself in his study. He was also afternoon preacher (1759–66) and Thursday lecturer (1766–7) at the Hanover Square church. His appointment as afternoon preacher in Clapham lasted from 1769 to 1775.

Savage was one of the first people whose appeal to Parliament in 1772 led to the 1779 amendment to the Toleration Act which replaced subscribing to the 39 Articles of the Church of England with a declaration of adhesion to the scriptures. He married twice: in 1752 to Mary, daughter of George Houlme, stockbroker of Hoxton Street, with whom he had two daughters, and secondly in 1770 to Hannah

Wilkin. Savage, an orthodox Calvinist, died of starvation on 21 February 1791, caused by contraction of the oesophagus. He was buried at Bunhill Fields. A 'Life of Samuel Morton Savage' is prefixed to *Sermons on Several Evangelical and Practical Subjects* published by Joseph Toulmin in 1796.

It is strange to note that one name not listed in the Clapham history of 1912 is that of Abraham Rees DD, one of the leading Presbyterian divines of his day. Rees was born in Llanbrynmair, Montgomeryshire, in 1743, the son of Lewis Rees (1710–1800), first minister of the Welsh Independent Old Chapel (Yr Hen Gapel) and later in Mynyddbach, Swansea. Abraham's mother was Esther Penry, a descendent of John Penry[8] the Dissenting martyr. In his article on John Penry in his *Cyclopaedia* Abraham Rees wrote, 'The editor of this *Cyclopaedia* traces his genealogy, by the maternal branch to the family of Mr Penry.'

After an education at a school kept in Llanfyllin by Dr Jenkin Jenkins (died 1780), Abraham Rees became a student at Coward's Academy (1759–62), being appointed assistant tutor in mathematics and natural philosophy in his final year. The academy moved to Hoxton in 1762, when he became resident tutor, and that until 1785. He served as a tutor in Hebrew and mathematics at New College, Hackney (1786–96). His first ministerial appointment was in Clapham, where he preached once a fortnight as an assistant to Philip Furneaux. Later he was pastor of the Presbyterian congregation at St Thomas', Southwark (1774–83) and at Old Jewry from 1783 until his death. Edinburgh University awarded him the degree of DD in 1775.

From 1778 Abraham Rees served for 60 years on the Presbyterian Board, and for 50 of those years as secretary, and later as president. He too was a member of the Dr Williams' Foundations from 1774 until his death in 1825. One of his appointments was that of principal distributor of HM Government's Annual Bounty to Indigent Dissenting Ministers (*Regem Donum*), a role he fulfilled with fairness for all, regardless of theology or churchmanship. Rees retained his contacts with Wales, in that he was a triennial examiner at the Carmarthen Presbyterian College. He was also a great and unbiased benefactor – both from his own pocket and other funds – to the needs of ministers in Wales, showing regard to those 'thought to be deserving of encouragement in their works of piety in their respective churches'.[9] He represented the General Body of Dissenting Deputies (of whom he was 'father'), on several occasions in their meetings with members of the government or the royal court, where he was always 'courteous, dignified, firm and upright'[10]. He was asked by the Deputies to present their loyal address and congratulations to two kings, George III and George IV, the only person so to do.

> In the former case, Lord Halifax, the Lord in Waiting, expressed a regret that Dr Rees did not belong to the right Church, for then his loyalty would be rewarded. He did not possess all the qualifications that the multitude would esteem in a Preacher; his were sterling merits: a sound and strong sense, a clearly-defined subject, well-digested thoughts, scriptural language, manly confidence in the affections of his auditory, and marked but sober earnestness. He practised no arts in the pulpit – on the contrary, he expressed his abhorrence of affectation, trick and mediated extravagance in a Christian minister... His Christian principles never forsook him. They had been the guide of his youth and the distinction of his middle age, and they were the stay of his old age.[11]

Another claim to fame was that he was the last of the Dissenting ministers to wear a wig when officiating.

Abraham Rees re-edited the *Cyclopaedia of Ephraim Chambers*, re-issued with a supplement in four volumes (1781–6). His own *The New Cyclopaedia or Universal Dictionary of Arts and Sciences... Biography, Geography and History &c.* in 45 volumes appeared between 1802 and 1820. In 1786 he was elected a Fellow of the Royal Society and later of the Linnean Society and the America Society. He died at his Finsbury home on 9 June 1825, in his 82nd year.

His obituary in the *London Literary Gazette* of that month, says:

> In his own religious community Dr Rees held a prominent rank.
> He was a Protestant dissenter upon principle, scrupling conformity
> to the Established Church both on the grounds of discipline and
> doctrines. In spirit he might be esteemed a Catholic Christian, if
> we learn from his worldly intercourse that no sectarian prejudices
> kept him aloof from the society of men of other denominations
> whose public or private worth entitled them to his esteem. He lived
> in terms of familiar intimacy with persons of all religious opinions,
> and reckoned among his most valued friends some of the brightest
> ornaments of the national church. He was an active and influential
> member of all the principal dissenting trusts in the Presbyterian
> connexion, and from his great age and early introduction into
> public life, had become the father of almost every institution to
> which he belonged.

Thomas Urwick became the minister in Clapham on 7
September 1778, receiving the votes of 27 subscribers out of
28. Born in Shelton near Shrewsbury on 8 December 1727,
he was the second son of Samuel Urwick, a member of an
old Shropshire family. Educated at Shrewsbury Grammar
School, he then went in 1747 to Philip Doddridge's Academy
in Northampton but, after Doddridge's death in 1751, he
completed his education at Glasgow University. He settled in
Worcester, serving as assistant minister at Angel Street church
from 1754, and sole pastor from 1764, being ordained in 1765.
Ten years later he moved to a small church in Narborough,
Leicestershire, where he laboured until his call to Clapham. He
succeeded Furneaux as a trustee of the Coward Trust and Dr
Williams' Foundations. He died on 26 February 1807.

Urwick was on good terms with the clergy of the Established
Church, in particular with John Venn, then rector of Clapham.
The Clapham Burial Register for 1807 lists him as, 'The
Revd Thomas Urwick. Aged 80. Pastor of the Dissenting
Congregation in this parish for many years.' There is no entry

for his wife, who died in 1791, though both are buried in the old churchyard. Their tomb, situated just north of the present St Paul's church in Rectory Grove, was smashed by vandals in 1967. Upon its restoration, the inscription, which had been illegible, was restored:

> Here are deposited the mortal remains of the Revd Thomas Urwick, during 26 years the able, faithful and beloved pastor of the Protestant Dissenting Church in this parish. Born, December 8th, 1727 and died after a short confinement, 26th February, 1807. Also the remains of his wife, Mary Urwick, who died 17th June, 1795, aged 65 years.

His obituary in the *Gentleman's Magazine and Historical Chronicle* Vol. 1 (1807), p. 282, reads:

> He might be called a Dissenter of the Old School; educated under Doddridge, he carried the principles of his tutor with him to the grave. Far removed from the Socinianism and semi-scepticism of many modern Dissenters, he gloried in maintaining the doctrines of Christianity, plainly, as he thought, revealed in the Gospel, and explained by Howe, Watts and Doddridge among the dissenters and divines of the Established Church... An ungraceful manner of delivery prevented his becoming a popular preacher, but he was most deservedly admired by those who frequented his ministry... he cultivated a friendly intercourse with the clergy of the Establishment.

At this time the Clapham Sect was in the process of formation. The Unitarian *Monthly Repository* attacked the above obituary, declaring that 'His religious opinions were by no means what we would call orthodox, nor could he, we apprehend, be justly said to believe in the Trinity in any sense.'

Whatever the perceived deficiencies of Urwick as a preacher, it became necessary during his ministry to add two new galleries to his meeting house. As was noted in the above obituary, he had a happy relationship with his

Anglican neighbours and it seems likely that it was at this time that the Congregationalists of Clapham moved away from the rationalism represented by Philip Furneaux and many of his assistants to a more orthodox Congregationalist and Trinitarian theology. This may have been affected by the Evangelical revival in general, but it may well be that the vibrant faith of Anglican neighbours of similar social background and outlook, and especially of the Clapham Sect, also played its part.

In 1795 Benjamin Carpenter of Stourbridge was elected co-pastor with Urwick, a post held by him until 1800. Carpenter was born around 1752 in Woodrow, near Bromsgrove. He was educated at Daventry Academy (1766–73), where he acted at tutor in the Classics for some months in 1773, prior to becoming pastor of the Congregational churches in Bloxham and Milton, Oxfordshire, where he was ordained in 1774. Two years later he moved to West Bromwich, where he remained for two years, before becoming a minister in Stourbridge (1778–95). After Clapham (1795–8), he served in Bromsgrove (1798–1807), before returning to Stourbridge (1807–16) where he died on 22 November 1816 aged 64.

The issue of the *Monthly Repository* containing Urwick's obituary also included an article entitled, 'Mr Belsham's Strictures upon Mr B. Carpenter's Defence of Arianism in his Lectures'. Nonetheless, it would appear that both Urwick and Carpenter were men of moderate views. A local historian described him thus:

> ... with good abilities, and talents highly respectable, improved by long and diligent application, were united in a spirit of habitual piety and seriousness. His candid and peaceable disposition, acknowledged by Christians of every denomination, his humility, meekness and patience &c, are likewise dwelt upon.'[12]

7

The Minute
Book of 1773

REFERENCE HAS BEEN made to the old Minute Book which was found in a black japanned box in 1968. A general meeting of subscribers to the new chapel in Clapham on 7 November 1782, drew up rules which 'contain many deviations from the strict theory of Independency'.[1]

At a meeting of subscribers to church funds (not a church meeting, incidentally), church officers were elected by subscribers. A minister was chosen by those whose names were recorded in the subscription book and who had paid their annual subscription for twelve calendar months before the meeting. The daily running of the church was in the hands of trustees who elected a committee and a treasurer. The only time in which all the subscribers would be summoned to meet would be for the election of a clerk or a minister, or when large expenditure on repairs was required.

These rules were revised on 27 May 1793 but, in Lovett's view, 'the revision leaves the constitution as oligarchical as ever'. In the Clapham historian's eyes, the situation went from bad to worse:

> The low water-mark is touched in a resolution of 30th July, 1806, 'that no person be allowed to vote for minister, clerk or pew-opener whose subscription do not amount to 2 guineas per annum.'
> Under the old rules, ladies subscribing in their own right were

empowered to vote in the choice of a minister by ballot in person, but on 7th February, 1791, it was resolved 'that the committee do recommend to the General Meeting to allow the Ladies subscribers to the Congregation to vote or ballot by proxy at the election of any minister or clerk.'

A committee of nineteen men was chosen to manage 'the affairs of the congregation'. They were given the power of co-option and there would be no further election to the committee by the subscribers. One of the committee's most delicate responsibilities was the allocating of pews, for which elaborate rules had been laid down in June 1761.

Trustees and managers had to subscribe a minimum of £25 per annum. Allocation of pews was in order of size of subscription, while every person subscribing £25 or upwards should 'have a right to a pew for himself, or herself, and family... That all ornaments and furniture be at the expence of each subscriber.' The right to keep pews was restricted to pew holders, their wives and lineal descendants, provided that they 'continue a stated subscription of no less than forty shillings a year to the minister.' Otherwise pews were not transferable. Remaining pews were allotted by the managers. In 1762 it was decided that anyone subscribing five shillings a year might rent a seat, but anyone subscribing less than twenty shillings a year must relinquish the seat on request. Complications could arise, as happened in 1804 when two prominent members applied for the same pew. In 1806 it was decided to extend this practice of 'taking sittings' from the ground floor of the chapel to the gallery. This practice continued into the twentieth century, and a letter typed by the Revd E. W. Lewis in 1907 refers to people 'taking sittings with us'.

The Minute Book also records the introduction of a second Sunday service by the subscribers' meeting of 2 February 1800, which resolved that 'in future, afternoon service should begin at 3.30 from Lady Day to Michaelmas, and at 3 from Michaelmas to Lady Day.' The practice of the early Independents was to keep

Sunday evening for quiet reading and meditation at home and for training the young, but many Congregational churches had already introduced evening services of an evangelical nature as a result of the influence of the Methodist Revival.

The Minute Book also records the decision of the subscribers on 16 February 1778 to set aside £80 for the care of Dr Furneaux in his illness, but this was reduced to £20 a year later in view of the size of the fund raised for his support. On 16 May 1806, it was resolved that the clerk's annual salary be sixteen guineas and that of the pew-opener, £13-4-0. The appointment of representatives to the Dissenting Deputies is also recorded, a practice which continued into the early twentieth century.

The Minute Book throws light on the sociological composition of the congregation – it contains more than one reference to the servants of subscribers. A deed of assignment of lease, dated 30 March 1764, and quoted in the Minute Book, contains the names of thirteen people acting for the church: four are described as 'Esquire', there is one 'merchant', one 'apothecary', and one 'linen draper of Cheapside', while two are 'cheesemongers of Thames Street'. Clapham had by this time become the residence of prosperous city gentlemen, both active and retired. The subscription list in 1761 reveals that five people subscribed £100 and another nine £50 or more.

The Minute Book is a mine of information about the building of a new meeting house. The church had grown so much under Dr Furneaux's ministry that by 1760 the Nags Lane meeting house was too small. 'At a general meeting of the subscribers to the support of the congregation of Protestant Dissenters at Clapham on Thursday, 4th June, 1761, at 6 o'clock in the evening', it was resolved to take a piece of land 'in the high street of Clapham, containing 120 feet in front and 340 feet in depth for 91 years from Michaelmas, 1761, at a rent of £12 per annum.' (The site, not in the present High Street, but on a corner where North Street, Grafton Square and The Pavement meet, was occupied in the late twentieth century by the headquarters of the National Union of Seamen.) The subscription list stood at £1,551-3-0. Lovett described it as 'a roomy brick building, plain and unadorned, with a gallery, and later a second gallery close to the ceiling. The congregation faced a wall with large windows on either side, and in the centre a lofty pulpit entered by a door through the wall. The organ was at the back of the church.'[2]

The congregation worshipped here until 1852 when the lease expired and the 'cathedral' around the corner in Grafton Square was erected. The first reference to a Sunday school appears on 4 April 1820, but it is clear that one had existed for very many years, as in 1803, a Miss Wilkinson offered to pay for the erection of semi-circular seats in the gallery for children. The meeting of 16 July 1820 resolved to rebuild and enlarge the girls' Sunday school and to build another school for boys at the end of the vestry.

8

Consolidation

FOR CLAPHAM'S DISSENTERS the new century was marked by the arrival of a new minister in the person of James Phillips of Haverfordwest, who was elected minister on 10 August 1800. Phillips was born in 1759 at Maenordy, Maenclochog, Pembrokeshire, and educated at Oswestry Academy. His first pastorate was at Barkway, Hertfordshire (1783–95). He kept an academy for ministerial students in Haverfordwest (1795–1800). John Waddington's *Surrey Congregational History* describes him as 'a man of urbane manner', adding that, his death in 1824 was 'deeply regretted by his Church and the whole neighbourhood'. Edward Cleal, author of *The Story of Congregationalism in Surrey*, speaks of him as 'a man of amiable disposition and universally loved'. The church subscribers' roll records 28 names on his arrival, with 92 others joining the church during his ministry.

George Browne became co-pastor with James Phillips in 1824 but, on the death of Phillips a few months later, he became sole pastor. Browne was born at Clapton on 14 February 1790. When the family moved to Hitchin he was educated at the school of the Revd F. Evans and joined the church there aged 17. Soon afterwards he suffered a serious illness and his mind turned to the ministry and he entered Rotherham Independent Academy in 1810. He was an assistant to Joshua Lambert in Hull until the latter's death in 1816. Browne rejected an invitation to become a tutor in the Classics in Rotherham. Instead he was ordained in St Albans in 1818, where he remained as minister of the church there until 1824, when he moved to Clapham.

In 1833 he became superintendent of the translating and editing department of the British and Foreign Bible Society, but continued to minister in Clapham for a further seven years until 17 May 1840 when he resigned from the pastorate to devote all his energies to the work of the Bible Society. The church presented him with £620 while 'the poor of the congregation gave him a silver salver'. Between the years 1854 and 1857 Browne wrote *The history of the British and Foreign Bible Society to the close of its Jubilee in 1854* in two volumes, and it was published in London in 1859.

He retired to Weston-super-Mare where he died in 1868. 'Browne is described as eminently a man of God. He was remarkable for his courteous bearing and his uniform kindness of disposition. He was of a calm and placid temperament, but was gifted with great firmness of purpose.'[1]

Browne was clearly an abstemious man as 'R. Lee's Private Cash Book, 1826', found in the black tin box, reveals. Roger Lee[2] was appointed 'Treasurer to Mr Browne's Meeting' in March 1826. He records that 'he gave a Bottle of Sherry Wine, for the use of the Minister in the Vestry', regularly until the end of 1829. On 11 January 1830, he adds, 'This is now discontinued by me and done with: the wine supply'd in the Vestry is paid out of the incidental expenses of the Congregation.' Mr Browne drank just nine bottles in a year.

However, the treasurer's notebook of 1849 reports: 'Given to the Minister out of mine own cellar each quarter day, twenty four bottles of the best claret.' On the notebook's first page records handed over to the new treasurer by his predecessor William Esdaile[3] were listed. These included four parchments, title deeds, leases etc. and one Roll or List of Original Subscribers to the Building (none of these has come to light), a Minute Book dated 1773, a Subscription Book (1798–1820), and a Minute Book and Cash Book, both for 1821–6. This reveals that even in 1726 none of the older books was extant. Since then the Minute Book of 1821–6 has disappeared.

There were also bundles of vouchers and letters from Mr Lee's period of office in the box, with some of the letters revealing disputes on how money was being spent. A particular nuisance to the treasurer seems to be one Mr Thomas Rogers, to whom Roger Lee writes on 11 February 1828, 'I have long considered you a troublesome person and beneath my notice, and should have continued to do so, had it not been for your intrusion at the Vestry Room of our Meeting a few evenings since...' It appears that Mr Rogers made a habit of turning up at meetings to object to items of expenditure, though he usually avoided making any contribution himself. The treasurer's life was made difficult by people who defaulted on their contributions, as the following letter blaming the government shows:

> Sir
> Consideration for my Family and Self will not allow of my giving anything away while the infamous quackery of free trade continues.
> Yours respectfully,
> Geo. Stevenson

In 1832 Roger Lee resigned and his letter to his successor, Stephen Williams, a lawyer, has survived:

> I am still ready and willing to do all I can for the Place, People and our worthy Minister, Mr Browne. I never can feel myself easy to be a leader of anything, out of my Family, I would rather be as the mole and work out of sight, or follow in any trail of usefulness. I am convinced none of us are sent into the world to be Idle.

In the latter years of his ministry Browne received ministerial assistance. The first assistant to be appointed was Edward Miller, who was born in Atherstone, Warwickshire, in 1785, the son of an army surgeon. His mother had died when he was five and his father when he was eleven, so he was raised by his grandfather, a clergyman in the Church of England. Educated at Christ's Hospital, Horsham, he entered the Civil Service in the Commissary General's department in 1804 at the age of 19, remaining there for 30 years. He became assistant pastor in Putney, where he was ordained in 1827, and remained there until 1835 when he joined George Browne in Clapham. Some sort of nervous breakdown caused him to resign and in August 1838 he accepted the temporary charge of a Chiswick church for three months. At the end of that period he was pressed to remain and a formal induction took place in December 1838. Under his ministry the Chiswick congregation grew, with benches being placed in every available space, including some free seats 'for the use of the labouring classes'. This increase in numbers and the short time remaining on the lease led the church, under his leadership, to build new premises. He remained in Chiswick until his retirement in 1850. He died on 28 June 1857.

Edward Miller was succeeded by a William Bean, who was born at Bridgewater, Somerset, on 19 November 1800, and ordained on 28 August 1827. The *Salisbury and Winchester Journal*, dated Monday, 3 September, reported:

> On Tuesday last the Rev. William Bean, was publicly ordained over the Independent Congregation at Whitchurch, Hants. A large concourse of people from the neighbouring towns and villages were convened on the occasion; and the Rev. Messrs. Jefferson of Andover, Adkins of Southampton, Good of Salisbury, Reynolds of Romsey, with several other ministers, conducted the interesting solemnity.

He served pastorates in Whitchurch, Hampshire (1827–8), 'where he conducted three services every Sunday,'[4] Hope Chapel, Weymouth (1828–36); Livesey Street, Birmingham (1836–9); Clapham (1839–40), where he was responsible for the Sunday evening lectures; Tulse Hill (1847–51); and Worthing (1855–63). (The *Surman Index* for Dissenting studies gives no information for the years 1840–7 and 1851–5.)

He became the second husband of Sarah Taylor and became the major beneficiary in the will of her uncle, William Bengo Collyer DD LLD (1782–1854),[5] who left him not only his collection of Philip Doddridge works and various biblical commentaries, but also 'all my leasehold houses lands and ground rents situate in Bath Place and all other my leasehold property at Peckham in the County of Surry to hold the same to him his executors administrators and assigns for his and their own absolute use and benefit,'[6] thus making him a wealthy and well-connected man. William Bean died on 14 November 1871. His obituary in the *Congregational Year Book* of 1872 says that he was 'distinguished by great kindliness and geniality of disposition. He was of a cheerful temper and always ready to help any friend, often at personal sacrifice. He had a commanding presence, great energy of character and a warm and brotherly heart.'

The next pastorate commenced in January 1841 with the arrival of James Hill. The black tin box contained a small book labelled 'Clapham Chapel 1840' containing details of a fund to provide £500 per annum for two years for a minister's stipend. The treasurer wrote: 'Clapham is well known to be an expensive place... In order to place a minister of suitable talent and standing over the Chapel at Clapham if he have a large family he would require £500 per annum'. As noted Clapham's Dissenters included many of the wealthiest families and the money was forthcoming.

James Hill was born in Stafford on 17 May 1795. Converted as the result of a sermon preached by the Revd W. Sylvester of Sandbach, he joined the Stafford church. Under the influence of its minister, James Chalmers, and then John Angell James, Hill decided to enter the ministry and trained at Gosport Academy.

He was accepted into the service of the London Missionary Society (LMS) and, after being ordained with two others at Hanley on 19 July 1820, he sailed to India to take up his appointment in Calcutta. Here, in 1822, he was invited to become the minister of Union Church, an expatriate congregation. After much heart-searching and with the approval of the LMS, he accepted, but did not turn his back on his original calling. 'The work was similar to that carried on in all great centres of population – English services, vernacular services, bazaar preaching, inquirers, educational work. Union Church has always been a centre of Christian work, self-supporting, and a liberal contributor to local funds.'[7]

A breakdown in his health necessitated Hill's return home in 1833. He then became minister of George Lane Chapel, Oxford, but this situation also caused health problems for the Hill family. They then moved to Salford where James was minister of Chapel Street from 1838 until his call to Clapham in 1840.

This was an eventful period in the life of the Clapham church, containing as it did the move from the High Street meeting house to a new building in Grafton Square. A building committee visited six churches before meeting with the architect, John Tarring. Nine tenders were received and the cheapest (£5,499) was accepted.

In volume six of *Brixton and Clapham Old and New London* (1878), Edward Walford says this of the Clapham churches:

> By far the finest ecclesiastical-looking structures at Clapham
> do not belong to the Established Church. These are the
> Congregational Chapel, in Grafton Square, built in 1852, one
> of the most commodious and elegant edifices of which London
> Nonconformists can boast; and the Roman Catholic Redemptorist
> Church of St Mary, built in 1849. These, with their lofty spires,
> quite dwarf the plain and unpretending parish structures.

The builder's bill and that for the Gray & Davison organ eventually came to £10,737-13-10. (This organ was sold to St John's Church, Buckley, some time later, and was moved to St Anne's Church, Worksop, by organ restorers Goetze & Gwynn in 1999.)

The official opening was held on Wednesday, 29 September

1852. Collections at the two services amounted to £145. The church had incurred a debt of over £3,000 but this sum was paid off by 1861.

James Hill was elected to the chair of the Congregational Union of England and Wales in 1860 and also served on the committee which prepared the *New Congregational Hymn Book*. In September 1861 he announced his retirement. The church membership of 110 in 1840 had reached some 300 by the time of his departure. The church granted him an annuity for life of £200, and £100 for Mrs Hill should she survive him. Hove became their retirement home, and he took on pastoral duties at the church there for another three years. He died in Brighton on 12 January 1870. 'Mr Hill's abilities were of a very high order. In manner he was dignified but attractive, as a speaker he was earnest and at times eloquent. Of his power at Clapham the facts speak.'[8] His retirement testimonial read that:

> ... he discharged the pastoral office among them with ability, faithfulness and acceptance – as a useful and earnest expositor of God's Word; as a helper of the devotional spirit and of the faith, hope and love of the children of God, as the comforter of many in the chamber of affliction; and as the guide of others in a state of ignorance and sin to the happiness which springs from faith in Christ Jesus.[9]

9

Nonconformist Might

WITH THE DEPARTURE of James Hill there followed a pastoral vacancy which lasted four years. Then, in February 1865, a subscribers' meeting issued an invitation to the Revd James Guinness Rogers to the pastorate, which he accepted the following month.

Guinness Rogers was born in Enniskillen, Fermanagh, on 29 December 1822, the son of Thomas Rogers and Anna Stanley. Both Thomas and Anna had been brought up as Anglicans. Thomas, a Cornishman, became a Congregationalist as a result of the influence of Thomas Wildlife of Falmouth. After training at the Irish Evangelical Academy, he became an agent of the Irish Evangelical Society. Anna, connected on her mother's side to the Guinness family, moved in 'refined circles' in Dublin society, but was led to associate herself with a small Independent chapel in that city.

Thomas and Anna had thirteen children, of whom only nine survived. Soon after the birth of James the family moved to Prescot near Liverpool, where Thomas became pastor of the Congregational church there. The local vicar tried to persuade Thomas to send James to Oxford but, like his father, the son would not renounce his nonconformity. Instead, he was educated at Silcoates School, Wakefield, and Trinity College, Dublin. Arthur Guinness, a first cousin of James' grandmother, paid for his education. In Dublin he often listened to Daniel

O'Connell, the Irish patriot, use his great gifts as an orator, and was touched by the man and his message.

After leaving Trinity College, Dublin, James proceeded to Lancashire Congregational College, which was based in Manchester, where he was the first student to enter his name on its books after its move from Blackburn. Once more his interests were not confined to his studies, for he frequented the Free Trade Hall where 'again and again I heard both Cobden and Bright, two orators from whom any young speaker might well receive invaluable lessons in his own special work in the pulpit.'[1]

In 1845 James Guinness Rogers accepted a call to St James' Church, Newcastle-upon-Tyne, where he spent six busy and happy years. It was here that he married Elizabeth, daughter of the Revd Thomas Greenall, minister of Bethesda, Burnley, in 1846. They were blessed with one daughter and three sons. All three sons followed their father into the Congregational ministry: Arthur Guinness Rogers DD, James William Rogers and Stanley Rogers. Their daughter Lilian married Alexander Mackintosh. A grandson, Frederic Chalmers Rogers MA, was chairman of the Congregational Union of England and Wales (1946–7).

James Guinness Rogers joined his friend Edward Miall in the Disestablishment campaign and was involved in forming a local branch of the British Anti-State Church Association, founded in 1844. (In 1853 it became known as the Society for the Liberation of Religion from State Control and Patronage, or Liberation Society.) In 1851 Rogers became minister at Ashton-under-Lyne, finding himself 'in the centre of a most energetic church' according to his autobiography. During his ministry there the Sunday school was rebuilt at a cost of £13,000. One of the first uses of the new building was to provide work for workers suffering because of the cotton famine. It was at this time that James Guinness Rogers' friendship with Dr Robert William Dale began, an alliance which lasted until their disagreement on the matter of the Irish Home Rule Bill more than 30 years later, strongly supported by Rogers and equally strongly opposed by Dale.

Then, in 1865, at the age of 43, Rogers became the minister of the Clapham church. His new pastorate was still semi-rural, with great mansions standing in their own grounds, the homes of wealthy city gentlemen interspersed with farmland and described as 'probably the congregation of the highest social standing in the denomination'.[2] It is worth quoting this long extract from the new minister's book, *J. Guinness Rogers: An Autobiography* (1903), in which he says this of Clapham:

> Clapham was as different from Ashton as Ashton was from
> Newcastle. I went to Ashton to try and maintain the honour and
> usefulness of a Church in its full strength. I went to Clapham to
> try and restore one which, during a four years' vacancy of the
> pastorate, had, so far as numbers were concerned, sadly fallen
> away from its high estate. 'We have nothing but a beautiful
> building to offer you' was a remark of one of the leading members
> when the 'call' was presented. It was too severe a depreciation of
> their position, but there was a strong element of truth in it. The
> church retained a strong nucleus of men, but in the absence of a
> pastor the congregation had dwindled. It was clear that it had to be
> restored almost from the beginning... Ere long I discovered men
> who, amid all the distractions of London life and the incessant
> calls of a society which had certain charms and duties too, for
> them, still kept warm and kindly hearts, and were prepared to give
> practical evidence that they meant to be true helpers of the new
> pastor whom they had invited. As might be expected in a suburb
> like Clapham, there were a considerable number of gentlemen who
> had either retired from business altogether or who had got to a
> period of life when they were working somewhat less strenuously
> than they had been accustomed in former years to do... They have
> all passed away long ago [in 1903], and their passing away – or
> rather the passing away of the class to which they belonged – has
> changed the whole character of the district to which I came nearly
> thirty years ago... Often as I cross the Common, I recall, in passing
> the various houses, or perhaps the sites of old mansions, where I
> used to be a familiar guest, the names of men well known in the
> Dissenting communities, and some of them considerably beyond,

men chiefly in the commercial classes, but including not a few others in public and Parliamentary life... The Clapham church had once the reputation of being an extremely aristocratic community. I was told that a leader of the working classes, who professed to be a Congregationalist, and to be interested in my ministry, was once asked to what church he belonged. 'Oh!' he said, 'I sometimes go to Grafton Square, but I can't stand the kid gloves. I can't understand how Mr Rogers stands them.' So far as I was concerned, I had nothing to stand.[3]

In the 1960s the church caretaker enjoyed recalling a piece of local folklore, namely that 'when the maid entered Dr Rogers' library to light the lamps, he took no notice because it was only the maid.' Guinness Rogers and his wife were both ardent total abstainers (despite their links with the Guinness family). She wrote that when they arrived in Clapham, 'we were horrified to learn that the ladies met every Thursday afternoon for sherry. But we soon put a stop to that.'

This period was one of expansion for the church led by James Guinness Rogers. It planted a new cause at Stormont Road, Lavender Hill, providing the first members and officers. A mission hall was built on the Wandsworth Road to serve the needs of this working-class neighbourhood. A Sunday school building was also erected close to Grafton Square.[4]

Rogers must have been a man of tremendous energy and commitment to be able to minister successfully to such a church and to take the prominent role he did in denominational and public affairs. He was active in the 1870 battle over education, holding at the time the belief that state sponsorship of – and financial support for – church schools, with the resulting control of religious education, was an evil, a view, incidentally, which he later modified.

In 1872 he addressed representatives of 800 Nonconformist churches, moving a resolution that they should not vote for any candidate who did not undertake to modify the 1870 Education Act. But all his hopes were dashed by the Conservative victory in the 1874 election. With his friend, R. W. Dale, he embarked on a

Revd J. Guinness Rogers
J.Guinness Rogers, An Autobiography (1903)

crusade for Disestablishment and together, in the winter of 1875, they addressed meetings in Bradford, Liverpool, Leeds, Manchester, Norwich and Derby, and finally a rally in London. Then, in the winter of 1876, they visited Hull, Bristol, Plymouth, Brighton, Newcastle-upon-Tyne, Swansea, Cardiff and Caernarfon. There were large audiences everywhere, but sometimes they faced egg-throwing opponents.

Shortly after arriving in Clapham, Rogers met the Liberal Party leader W. E. Gladstone at a soiree at the home of the Revd Dr Christopher Newman Hall. A deep friendship began between the two men and Gladstone used Rogers as an unofficial commentator on Nonconformist opinion. They enjoyed regular correspondence: in a letter in 1892, Gladstone wrote, 'It is certainly interesting to note the supreme deference which today is made to public opinion. The result is not always one in which we can rejoice.'[5] Rogers gave strong support to Gladstone on the 'Eastern Question' and particularly the Bulgarian atrocities.

It was in the drawing room of Dr Rogers' residence that Gladstone launched his Home Rule for Ireland campaign in 1892, before proceeding to address a crowd from the balcony.[6] This move on the part of the Prime Minister divided both the Liberal Party and Nonconformists. Many turned against Gladstone and supported the Liberal Unionists, including, as has been noted, Dr R. W. Dale. It is clear that Rogers shared their concern about the peril of splitting the Empire and the dangerous position of Irish Protestants, especially in Ulster, but he remained loyal to the Prime Minister. As David Bebbington puts it in *The Nonconformist Conscience* (1982): 'The magic of Mr Gladstone kept back Rogers from the brink of opposing home rule.'[7]

Guinness Rogers was also friend of the 5th Earl of Rosebery[8] who consulted him as the leading representative of Nonconformist feeling. However, Rogers' loyalty to Gladstone appears to have been limited to the world of politics, as *The Spectator* of 13 June 1896 reports:

> The Rev. J. Guinness Rogers preached a strong sermon last Sunday evening (the 7th inst), at the Clapham Congregational Church on Mr Gladstone's letter, taking as his text St Paul's exhortation to the Galatians, 'Be not entangled again in the yoke of bondage.' The positive drift of the sermon was that Mr Gladstone's plea for unity had 'mistaken the mechanical for the dynamic force which was behind the gospel of Christ'. If Mr Rogers only means that in attaching so much importance to the recognition or non-recognition of Anglican orders by a Church which holds the Anglican Church to be heretical, Mr Gladstone appears to subordinate matters of substance to matters of form, we should agree with him. But when he adds that anything tending to reunion 'could not take place without certain concessions on the part of the Anglican Church, and if submission were made to the Pope, it would be admitting in the face of Christendom that the Reformation was an egregious mistake and an impertinent anachronism.' We cannot help regarding his address as itself an anachronism unless he can produce proof that any such submission is really contemplated by any important number of the Anglican clergy. Is there the smallest evidence of this? Mr Guinness Rogers and Dr Parker seem to us to have got Romanising on the brain.

***

In his article in the *Methodist Times* of February 1890, Guinness Rogers had called for 'a congress of Free Churches' which would present the essential unity of the Free Churches. This led to a private meeting of leading ministers which, in turn, resulted in the first meeting of the Free Church Congress in Manchester in 1892. But, Rogers, a great believer in individualism, disassociated himself from it when it became a representative body. He was also involved in the founding of the International Congregational Council and was elected a vice-president at its first meeting in 1891.

Despite all these demands on his time and energy, Rogers ensured that it was his denomination which had first claim upon his time, after his church in Clapham. He was chairman of the Lancashire Congregational Union in 1865, the Surrey Congregational Union in 1869, and the London Congregational Union in 1879. In 1874 he was elected chairman of the Congregational Union of England and Wales. The Clapham church also provided other leading figures for the Congregational Union of England and Wales: W. Marten Smith was its treasurer from 1874 to his death in 1912. Rogers also assisted Dale in the founding of *The Congregationalist* magazine, succeeding him as editor in 1878.

By 1890 Guinness Rogers accepted a less strenuous life. That year Edinburgh University conferred on him an honorary DD. This was also the 25th anniversary of his arrival in Clapham. The church presented him with a cheque for 1,100 guineas, while Mrs Rogers received a silver tea service.

Five years later, in 1895, he asked the church to provide an assistant to help him with his ministry, and James Wilberforce Sibree, a student at Cheshunt College, Hertfordshire, was appointed in 1896. Sibree, a member of a great missionary family, was born at Ambohiamge, Madagascar, on 13 August 1871, the son of James Sibree DD. Sibree stayed in Clapham for two years, making his mark especially among the young people, before being appointed by the LMS as a missionary to Samoa in 1898. Retiring from Samoa in 1921 because of ill-health, he became minister of Epping Congregational Church, Sydney, New South Wales. His brother and three sisters also served as LMS missionaries, as did some of their descendants.

This was a period of growth and expansion. When Guinness Rogers arrived, the membership was around 300, but when he retired it was three times that number, with congregations swollen by large numbers of adherents and visitors too. He'd commenced his ministry in Clapham on an annual stipend of £600 and this became £1,000 before he retired on 25 January 1900, exactly 35 years after his first visit to Clapham. The church presented him with a testimonial and another cheque for £1,100, while Mrs Rogers received a diamond and sapphire ring. He remained active for some years until weakening sight and growing feebleness defeated him. Mrs Rogers died in 1909, followed by her husband on Sunday, 20 August 1911, in his 89th year.

Rogers had retained his membership of the Clapham church until the radical theology of his successor caused him to withdraw. Rogers' loud opposition to the New Theology (which attempted to re-interpret the Gospel using the language and ideas of contemporary philosophy, something which was also espoused by the minister of the prestigious City Temple, R. J. Campbell) was reported across the world, as items in two New Zealand newspapers reveal. Both the *Otego Witness* and the *Putanga Star* carried reports on the subject in January 1907. The former noted two accounts received 'by electric telegraph' from London under the headline, 'The New Theology: Rev. R. J. Campbell rebuked – Rev. R. J. Campbell forms a League.' And that of January 15 states, 'The Rev. J. Guinness Rogers, an eminent Nonconformist divine, and others have severely rebuked the Rev. R. J. Campbell's heterodoxy,' while yet another adds, 'the Rev. R. J. Campbell of the City Temple, supported by some Nonconformist and Anglican clergy and laymen, has formed a New Theology League.' The article ends with, 'The Rev. J. Guinness Rogers is 82 years of age, and was for 35 years minister of Clapham Congregational Church. He is an Irishman, a Liberal and an untiring advocate of Free Church principles.'

***

The years of Dr Rogers' ministry had been a period of development and outreach. After leaving the old meeting house, the church lost its Sunday school rooms and from 1852 the Sunday school met in the Church Parlour. But another Sunday school building was erected at Belmont Road, together with the Mission Hall at Queen's Place, Wandsworth Road. The church also built Milton Hall, Battersea, in 1873, with the help of a £500 cheque from Samuel Morley MP, and maintained 'the special work for the classes of the people who do not normally come into the ordinary places of worship,'[9] In 1880, two members, 'Mr Hamilton and Mr Clegg applied to the deacons for authority to carry on an evening service at Queen's Place' and that service continued to be held up until the publishing of Lovett's history of the church in 1912.

The aim of all this activity was to serve and evangelise the working-class population of the Wandsworth Road and Battersea areas without bringing them to Grafton Square. Half a century later a minister's attempts to merge these led to great pain. Then came the founding of a splinter church in Lavender Hill which opened in February 1886. An institute building came later, in 1904, containing a billiard room and another comfortable room. Building and furnishing costs came to £600, half of which was provided by Clement Colman (of mustard fame) and a Mr Clegg.

Lovett ends *A History of Clapham Congregational Church* with a note about the church's music. The 1852 organ cost £445-7-0 and it underwent extensive refurbishment in 1880. This instrument was replaced by a Hunter organ, at a cost of £700 in 1902. John Post Attwater FRCO (1862–1909) served as organist from 1886 until his death in 1909. Clement Colman

(1851–1913) was the choirmaster, and the Clapham church was the only Free Church in England with a choir of boys (who wore Eton suits) while the men were clad in tail coats. The boys were paid half-a-crown a week and the leading singer's voice was trained at Colman's expense.

Colman exercised strict control over the boys, being known to hit them over the head with his hymn book if they made a noise during the service. In 1886 Novello, Ewer & Co. published his *The Clapham Chant and Anthem Book* at a cost of four shillings per copy. The church's organists in this period were all musicians of skill and substance, in keeping with its great musical tradition. Colman also became church treasurer in April 1906.

10

The New Theology

THE CHURCH TOOK two years to find a suitable candidate to succeed Guinness Rogers. They were probably seeking someone who was as dynamic as Rogers had been when he was called. In 1902 the Revd Edward Williams Lewis MA BD was elected minister. Born in Middleton-by-Youlgrave, Derbyshire, the son of the Revd Matthew Lewis (1832–97), a Congregational minister, he was educated at Caterham School, Surrey; Lancashire Congregational College and London University. His previous pastorates were Hamilton Square, Birkenhead (1896–8) and Swan Hill, Shrewsbury (1898–1902).

A former church deacon, John Drennan[1], described Lewis as:

> ... a tall man of striking appearance, with a shock of gray hair. He was one of the finest preachers I ever heard. He was a profound thinker and, though his style was unemotional and undemonstrative, with a magnificent voice, the logic, development and intellect displayed in his sermons was most convincing and edifying. At that time he was engaged, with Dr R. J. Campbell of the City Temple, in explaining the 'New Theology' as it was called, an attempt to divest the Gospel of legend and superstition which is still being made today to make religion understandable to the young, educated but cynical masses.

Lewis was a keen Liberal who declined an invitation to be the parliamentary candidate for Clapham. He was an enthusiastic advocate of total abstinence. This example of his writing comes from the church manual in 1907:

78

This discrepancy, therefore, between the conclusions and
suggestions of modern thought and the creeds and the teaching of
the Church, calls aloud for some remedy and re-adjustment. And
we cannot put back the shadow of the dial even in the interests
of the Church. Every time the Church has said, 'Conform to me',
she has suffered; and if the Church adopts this attitude towards
modern thought, her only answer will be the voices of mocking
laughter above the quick waters. The Church can no more resist
the onflow of modern thought than Mrs Partington of Sidmouth,
could keep back the tempestuous Atlantic from her kitchen door
with a mop-cloth and a pail. The imperative demand therefore is
for a re-statement of the creed, the doctrine, the theology of the
Church. And there is no reason why we should be pessimistic. A
living truth can always be re-stated in a new form without loss;
not a hair on your head shall perish. It is possible to express in
full conformity with the received results of modern thought, and
with a triumphant persuasiveness, the fundamental, essential
faith and gospel of Christianity. Some of the old forms will have
to go...

However Lewis' ministry offended many church members,
including five prominent deacons, all of whom resigned
their membership. Church income also fell. A special church
meeting was called on 10 January 1907. The minutes record a
letter from a Mr Highton who announced his resignation from
the diaconate because 'he felt it impossible to continue to hold
office as deacon because of the views held by Mr Lewis, views
which the writer considered quite contrary to those which he
was invited to the pastorate of this church to maintain.'

Mr W. Marten Smith, the church treasurer,

... held that the fourth sermon on the 'New Theology' so
accentuated the chairman's views [the minister was in the chair]
that there could be no doubt as to the doctrine he was proclaiming
and considered that it was wholly opposed to that which Mr Smith
presumed he accepted when he undertook the pastorate of this
church and which till then, he presumed, to be the doctrinal basis
of the Clapham Congregational Church.

Revd Edward W. Lewis

Another deacon, a Mr Glegg, then spoke and explained that his term of office did not expire until 31 December 1909, but that he now tendered his resignation to the church. His reason for taking this step was 'Mr Lewis' divergence of belief on some of the fundamental doctrines as held essential by the Evangelical Free Churches'. Mr Glegg wished to make it quite clear to his fellow members that:

... he had not parted from Mr Lewis, but that Mr Lewis had parted from him. Mr Lewis had diverged at so marked an angle and so great a speed, that... he would recede farther and farther from the main line of the religious beliefs on which our church life had been running. To mention one divergence only: Mr Lewis is disputing the Deity of Christ, crossed over from the Evangelical Free Churches and took up a Unitarian position.

In Mr Glegg's opinion 'Mr Lewis had also gone beyond the terms of the church's trust deed, after allowing the widest latitude in interpreting its clauses.'

A Mr Sellar then spoke and stated that he, like his colleagues, felt bound to differ from Mr Lewis' teaching on points which he considered fundamental. The following resolution was made:

That this meeting of the members of Clapham Congregational Church tenders its hearty thanks to Messrs. F. J. Butcher, A. Glegg, E. G. Highton and W. M. Smith for their long and valued services on the diaconate and desires to place on record its deep regret at the severance of their connection with the church in that capacity. Moved by Mr Colman and seconded by Mr Adams who regretting the step their friends had felt themselves obliged to take from conscientious motives and taking the opportunity whilst speaking to express their own high appreciation of Mr Lewis' teaching.

It was at this time too that Dr James Guinness Rogers and his wife left the church. The way in which the Clapham congregation moved from the Victorian evangelicalism of the pastor who led it for half a century, to the liberal theology of his successor, is surely not unique. Churches often surprise observers in the seemingly casual way in which they call their pastors, without too much enquiry into their theology or churchmanship. It needs to be said that those Clapham church members still active in the 1960s remembered this period with great warmth and affection, and it seems likely that this 'most convincing and edifying' minister with his profound thought, logic and intellect had a tremendous influence on those who heard him or read his writings.

At the start of the twentieth century pew-rents were 7/6 a quarter in the gallery and £1-1-0 a quarter in the body of the church. In the 1960s two elderly ladies recalled this period: Miss Winifred Turner spoke glowingly of the minister's children's addresses, treasuring a published copy of them. Living in the shadow of Brixton Prison, she remembered, 'Daddy, putting on his frock coat, his gray gloves and his top hat; then picking up his walking cane or umbrella to walk across the Common on Sunday afternoon to attend the Brotherhood meeting.'

The other lady, Mrs E. M. Ware, recalled that her brother's four-figure membership card for the Brotherhood began with the number 1,300. She described how she was a member of the church at Battersea Bridge Road at this time and leader of its Girls' Friendly Society (GFS). She was engaged at the time to a young Mr Ware and they would accompany his mother to R. J. Campbell's Wednesday lunch-time services. One evening she was summoned to meet the deacons of her church, who sat solemnly around a table as she stood before them. They asked whether it was true that she attended meetings at Mr

Campbell's church. On receiving an affirmative reply, they informed her of their opinion that she was 'not a fit person to have the care of young people'. She turned on her heel and left. When she turned up for her GFS meeting, she discovered that the locks had been changed. She and her fiancé moved to the church in Grafton Square in late 1907. Later she applied to Battersea Bridge Road for a letter of transfer. The church secretary's reply read, 'If you wish to go to the devil, you will do so without our help.'

According to John Drennan, elected deacon in 1926, later becoming church treasurer, 'the church became more democratic under Mr Lewis, its politics definitely veered to Liberal, and Mr Lewis was asked to stand as the Liberal candidate for Clapham [in 1906] but declined.'

It was during Lewis' ministry that the church magazine *Grafton News* was introduced in 1907 (handsomely-bound copies from the beginning were kept in the vestry in the 1970s). Lewis eventually persuaded the deacons to hold a social hour after the evening service. Their reservations melted away when, as the church secretary wrote of the first such event, 'a goodly number of the right sort of people turned up'. Lewis also introduced an attempt at postal evangelism in 1904, when it was decided to post 1,500 cards each month to local residents, inviting them to services. The church was home to a great number of activities, including a cycling club of 300 members. Lewis was a committed supporter of total abstinence as well.

The famous black box contained carbon copies of letters written by him to the church secretary who was on a round-the-world cruise at the time for the sake of his health. In them he gives detailed descriptions of the church's life at the time. In one letter he records the arrival at church one Sunday morning of 'a coach drawn by four horses, with powered flunkies (How I abominate this kind of thing!). The coach belonged to a Mrs Watney of the Distillery, Wandsworth. The name speaks for itself. I wonder how she will cope with my temperance sermons.

Still, if she could put up with Dr Myers at Christ Church, she can put up with me.'

The May 1976 edition of *Grafton News* contained this article entitled 'Vanished World' by Miss Hilda Drennan (sister of John Drennan), aged 80 at the time of writing.

In 1906 our family moved to London – to Clapham, then a popular suburb with a very busy High Street lined with thriving shops. It could support three biggish drapery stores (Barratts, Richd. Williams and Lamings) and opposite the 'Plough', the clock tower had been recently set up to commemorate a year as Mayor of Wandsworth and a Knighthood by one of the Grafton Square deacons.

The reason for our removal had been the death of my father in the previous August and it was thought best to unite the family in London where my eldest brother and sister had lived and worked for some years. So, after settling in our new home in Elms Road, we were ready to try out our new Church in Grafton Square! It was customary for the bereaved to observe full mourning for at least one year and it was rather a sombre procession which crossed the Common that fine May morning. All were dressed completely in black, but being ten years old my youth excused me and I was allowed a dress of black and white check with a leghorn hat trimmed with black ribbon bows.

The Church we were going to was the fine stone building with its tall spire, built in 1851. Its interior was fitted with polished wooden pews and its gallery could seat over 1,000 worshippers. Income was derived from pew rents and the centre pews were the most expensive and the most sought after. Each pew had its cushioned seat, strip of carpet, hassocks and a box holding bibles and hymn books. We had a front pew in the gallery which gave me a splendid view of the congregation as well as the latest fashions. The Church was full; the sidesmen were moving to and fro showing strangers to their seats; the Choir was in its place – two rows facing each other on either side of the pulpit – boys in front and men behind. Unlike most Nonconformist Churches, this was an 'all male' choir presided over by Mr Clement Colman (of the mustard family) whose main interest it was. He personally paid the boys and selected the special soloist and, as there was a talented

musician at the organ (Mr J. P. Attwater, Mus. Bac) the music was
of a high order.

On the stroke of eleven, preceded by his Senior Deacon,
the Rev. E. W. Lewis MA BD emerged from the Vestry and swept
into the pulpit. He looked very tall as he stood in his silk gown
and scarlet hood waiting to begin. His was a great following of
young people and the service always contained a Children's hymn
and address, for Mr Lewis was a splendid story teller – some of
his stories were later published in book form. And so the service
continued with chant, anthem and sermon until well after noon.
Morning Service over, the people came out into the sunshine,
greeting friends and gathering into groups to discuss the sermon.
Our family was soon absorbed, for everyone was very sociable
and I too had some success as my strong Scottish accent caused
amusement and I was given invitations to tea when my hearers
would have more time to understand what I said!

Suddenly the general stir ceased as the Minister and
his family emerged from the Church and the ranks of the
Congregation parted to let them pass. Theirs was almost a royal
progress, with bowing and doffing of silk hats on every side. Mr
Lewis seemed to tower above everyone. Mrs Lewis was most
elegantly dressed and behind them trotted their son, Cecil, later
to become Uncle Caracticus of BBC *Children's Hour*. He was
dressed in an Eton suit with a miniature silk hat on the back of
his head and looking very much ashamed of the 'rig' he was made
to wear.

This family was making its way to their comfortable home
in The Chase where there were at least two maids in the kitchen.
Mr Lewis received a stipend of £600 a year – a princely sum in
those days and could well afford to keep up a good establishment,
dress his wife expensively and ensure keeping up with current
ideas by investing in learned books to line his study's shelves. And
so we dispersed to our homes – some taking the 'Church Parade'
along the sides of the Common en route. This was a pleasant and
colourful sight and provided a free Pageant – the ladies in their
silk gowns and feathered hats and boas escorted by their frock-
coated men folk.

A lot is said of dismal Victorian Sabbaths, but we knew
nothing of that at Grafton Square and looked forward eagerly
to the first day in the week. It was busy with two services and

Sunday school in between but it was a 'special' day. Mothers provided the best dinner and nicest tea of the week and all had some sort of 'Sunday Best'. Some too got their full quota of clean clothing that morning, so cleanliness was certainly next to Godliness!

Don't say it was all vanity and people went to Church for the wrong reasons. Some certainly did but they had to join in the hymns (most men then could sing a tenor or bass part) and sit still and listen to wise and beautiful words. At least the tensions of the week were broken and at best what was heard could remain with them all their lives. And surely it was a compliment to God that ordinary people put on their best to visit his House?

***

In October 1909 Lewis penned his farewell letter in *Grafton News*, saying that 'Happily we remain in earshot; within call of each other; and in so far as the new arrangements will permit, any call you make to me to serve you in any way will find me readier than, I think, for anything else in the world.'

The Clapham pastor left to go to Kings Weigh House church in 1909 to begin a joint ministry with R. J. Campbell, minister of the City Temple, in an arrangement which specified that Lewis would be minister and pastor of the church, while Campbell resided in the parsonage and conducted regular weeknight services. The City Temple guaranteed both stipends for a period of three years. Lewis held this position until the spring of 1914, when he wrote a letter of resignation, sent from Assisi, Italy. In this he stated that, 'I have felt for some time the incongruity between the possibility of being a man of God and the possibility of being a comparably high salaried and comfortably conditioned officer in organised religion.'[2] It has already been noted that the minister was uncertain of his own beliefs.

Lewis entered journalism and became an agnostic. R. J. Campbell had left Kings Weigh House church in 1912, and in 1915 he joined the Church of England. The New Theology movement, born within English Congregationalism, thus lost its leader and one of his chief lieutenants. Among Lewis' published works is *The Inescapable Christ and other sermons (An Expression of the New Theology)* published in 1907.

The October 1909 issue of *Grafton News* also carried an article headed, 'The Rev. E. W. Lewis: an impression,' written by 'a member of the Church and the Men's Meeting':

I still vividly remember the first time I ever heard Lewis preach. A friend of mine said to me, 'I'm going to church, will you come?' I laughed, for church going had long since ceased to be a habit of mine; I believe I declined, but my friend went on, 'I'm going to hear Lewis, he's no ordinary parson, I assure you; tells you straight what he thinks and means it too: he's not afraid of telling his people he doesn't believe in hell-fire – and all that...' I believe my friend made an utterance of essential truth. He had not only realised that Lewis was a man of intellect, he had realised his courage, his sincerity, his hatred of cant, his quarrel with the dry bones of traditionalism: what neither of us then could perceive was the deep spirituality of the man – that took us time – for we had for years been drifting towards materialism. Well, together we went 'to hear Lewis.' I went partly reluctant, partly curious, partly patronising. On entering the church, I recall being pleasantly impressed by the building, horribly oppressed by the pervading air of respectability. When, at length, Lewis's head appeared above the cushion of the high pulpit, I must confess to a feeling of disappointment. I liked the tall, athletic build of the man, but I was not attracted by the face. I whispered to my friend, 'He's not exactly what the girls would call nice-looking.' His face seemed to me stern and forbidding, somewhat heavy and pugnacious and, like a fool, I jumped to the conclusion, 'I've come here to be rated by a sulky dogmatist.' Everyone knows I was wrong – ridiculously, childishly wrong – but my purpose is simply to record my impressions just as I recall them – may I plead in extenuation that the light was dim and religious. I have a somewhat distinct recollection of his hair – not so grey then as it is now. I recall too his trick of pushing those long, nervous fingers of his through it; his abrupt, almost curt manner of announcing the opening hymn. I rather fancy the service bored me, I half believe I should have slipped out but, luckily, I was well up in the body of the church, and my way out of the pew was barred by a portly matron, on whose toes I should have had to tread. Dear old lady, I owe her much!

And then the sermon! It was a revelation – clear and logical in style, quiet and earnest in delivery, revealing unexpected stores of humour, tenderness and sweet reasonableness, it seemed to me pregnant with calm and strong enthusiasm, backed by tremendous moral force. I was deeply impressed, both by the man and his message – the thing seemed real. I do not know how else to express it. This was not the usual pulpit 'pap' I had been accustomed to have served up to me. Here was a grown man, one who understood my intellectual difficulties and could sympathise with them. This was no mere pietist, no mere 'literary' sermoniser, no human gramophone propounding traditional doctrines from traditional texts in the traditional way. Above all, the preacher stood for something definite; he gave me a foothold.

And so I came away feeling helped, comforted, uplifted. I had entered the church imagining Christianity was a dead thing; but this man rolled away the stone from the sepulchre, and unloosened the grave clothes with which 'orthodoxy' had bound Jesus; and though some might utter that pitiless, faithless cry, 'they have taken away the Lord', to me it was restoration, resurrection. So I came again and again, until now – thank God for Lewis!

Edward Carpenter (1844–1929), socialist prophet, poet and gay activist, says in his autobiography, *My Days and Dreams* (1916) of Lewis in his King's Weigh House period:

My friend Edward Lewis, himself a writer on the New Theology, was in 1912 and 1913 minister of the King's Weigh House Church, Duke Street, W., and he and R. J. Campbell not unfrequently interchanged pulpits at that time. Lewis persuaded me to speak at his church; and on two occasions (November 1912 and October 1913) I did so. His congregation, largely trained no doubt and educated by his discourses, was an intelligent and sympathetic one, and though I had some misgivings on my first visit in speaking on so abstruse a subject as 'The Nature of the Self' – illustrated as it was by numerous quotations from the *Upanishads* and from *Towards Democracy* – I felt no misgiving on the second occasion, when my subject (similarly illustrated) was 'Rest'. These lectures were repeated at the Lyceum (women's) Club, Piccadilly, at Croydon, Eastbourne, and elsewhere; and the fact that audiences like these, of a rather popular character, could listen with deep understanding and sympathy to the unfolding of innermost psychological teachings has convinced me that the germs of a new and democratic religion are only waiting among our mass-peoples for the day and the stimulus which will bring them to birth and development. Edward Lewis, being vigorous in heart and brain, and a real man, naturally could not continue very long in a profession like 'the ministry', which entailed his ascending the pulpit three or four times a week and not only giving 'edifying' counsel to his congregation but confining his own life within a corresponding circle of inanity. Such a career would inevitably have sapped and ruined his manhood; and with true instinct he threw up his five or six hundred a year and retired into the wilderness. The members of his congregation were duly shocked and grieved in their different ways, according to the views they took of his lapse or lapses from holiness; but if, as is likely, the quondam Christian minister should become the missionary and apostle of a new and vital Paganism, the world will be very much the gainer.

11

A Busy Church

AN EXAMINATION OF church manuals from the early years of the twentieth century show that the Clapham church operated on three sites: the large church situated in Grafton Square, boasting the tallest spire in south London and a Parlour for weekday meetings; the Mission Hall down the hill on the Wandsworth Road; and the Belmont Hall on Belmont Road, Clapham.

The church took great pride in its 54th London Company of the Boys' Brigade, with A detachment meeting at the Wandsworth Road Mission Hall and B detachment at Belmont Hall. In June 1902, a total of 99 boys were members. In the 1960s the church possessed photographs of the Boys' Brigade being inspected by the Duke of Cambridge in Hyde Park.

Belmont Hall served the London side of the Grafton Square area. On Sundays this was the home of a children's service and a Boys' Brigade Bible class at 10.30 a.m., with afternoon Sunday school (200 children in 20 classes in 1903; 195 in 1906). In 1903, 110 of the children were also members of the International Bible Reading Association. By 1906 the 'Tamate Missionary Band' had been formed, with 63 children subscribing to *News from Afar* (LMS). On weeknights, its doors opened for meetings of the Boys' Brigade and the Girls' Guild (with its drilling and singing), as well as a Penny Bank[1] on Tuesdays.

The Sunday evening service at the Mission Hall, Wandsworth Road, had been introduced in 1882, with an average attendance of 100 in 1903. In 1907 a monthly Lantern Service was introduced in an attempt to attract more people. There was a children's service at 10.30 am. (with an attendance of 80–100 in 1903). The afternoon Sunday school had 400 children on its books in 1903, with an average attendance of 300, meeting in 22 ordinary classes, five senior classes and an infant class of about 100. Fifty-five Girls' Guild members met weekly for 'Musical Drill and Sewing'. A library was added in 1907. Between 70 and 100 attended the Band of Hope. Pleasant Wednesday evenings were introduced in 1902. The 1903 manual invited 'any lady or gentleman who can sing, recite or play, to cheer and brighten many a weary heart after a hard day's toil.' By 1908, this had been replaced by an afternoon Women's Own meeting, with an average attendance of 120. A Men's Meeting had also been started.

On Sunday afternoons, the church parlour was home to the children's happy hour, which consisted of a Bible class for boys and girls. The Guild 'for the purpose of social intercourse, mutual improvement and comradeship among the Young People in attendance at the services of the Church' was founded in October 1902 and met on Monday evenings. The membership of 200 'had meetings of a varied character and, of which the arrangements were entirely in the hands of the young people.' The Young People's Society of Christian Endeavour (founded 1897), meeting on Tuesday evenings for an open weekly prayer meeting, numbered twenty active, five associate and 24 honorary members. The Sibree Band or the Children's Missionary Society, named after a former assistant minister who became a missionary in Madagascar, held a monthly Saturday afternoon meeting, where girls engaged in needlework and boys in wood carving and iron bending to contribute to the children's stall at the ladies' Sale of Work.

The parlour was also the meeting place for several organisation concerned with good works. The Ladies' Missionary Working Society for Home Objects (changed later to The Ministers' Aid Society) held fortnightly gatherings, where boxes of clothing were collected to help the families of ministers in rural charges, whose stipends were small. The Ladies' Benevolent Society's principal object 'was the relief of the poor during sickness with food and coals in and around the Wandsworth Road'. It employed a Bible Woman, who 'is a very earnest and diligent worker among these poor folk, and greatly interested in her work, assisting each member of a family whose needs she fully enters into, and many are the ways in which she helps them.' These included helping girls get work, getting people into hospital and visiting them there and supplying clothing, shoes and boots. In 1907 the Ladies' Benevolent Society was linked with the Mission Hall evening services and the Women's Own 'so that a united front should be waged against the evils of the slum-land that surrounds the Queens Road Mission Hall.'

The Dorcas Society, founded in 1884/5, made 'useful garments' for the poor 'which are sold at a very low price.' The LMS' Watchers' Band, which existed to support two missionaries, had 86 members. The church had its own auxiliary of the LMS, representative of all the church's missionary organisations. In 1902 it contributed £635-3-9 to the LMS.

The Total Abstinence Society had shared in the twentieth-century Temperance crusade and held joint monthly meetings with the local Baptist church. But in January 1906 members of the society voted unanimously 'That, because of the lack of support of the total abstaining members of the congregation, the Society feels that it cannot carry on its work any longer. The members wish to put on record their extreme regret that this step has been rendered necessary.'

The Men's Society (remembered in the 1960s by two ladies as the 'Brotherhood') was founded in 1903 by Edward W. Lewis and grew at remarkable speed. Before long a number of organisations operated under its auspices. Its main event was the Sunday Afternoon Meeting, 'always a bright swinging service.' Among the speakers were a Buddhist monk Bhikka

Ananda Metteyya, Annie Bessant (on 'Unseen World') and Dr Saleeby (on 'The sublimation of sex'), Mrs Charlotte Despard, and Mrs Philip Snowdon (on 'Women's Suffrage'), Liberal MPs Robert Laidlaw (on 'The Opium Question') and Hamar Greenwood, Labour politicians such as Arthur Henderson and John Hodge (both became Labour cabinet ministers), historian G. M. Trevelyan (on 'Garibaldi'), John Turner from the Shop Workers' Union (on 'The Living-in System'), and Jaakoff Prelooker (on 'The Reform Movement in Russia'). Other subjects included Congo Reform, Sweated Industries, the House of Lords and the Virgin Birth.

A monthly men's prayer meeting was held in the church parlour on Wednesday evenings and there was an adult Bible class in the church parlour on Sunday mornings at 9, with 'the first half hour devoted to a discussion of some matter of interest to members; the subjects vary from motor cars to heredity; the following hour is devoted to studying the Bible in a frank, open way. The class is conducted on conventional lines, and is very useful.'

A male voice choir was formed to lead the singing at the Sunday afternoon service. A book club 'helped men save money for the purpose of buying books'. The employment bureau helped unemployed members find work, the Slate Club (through its subscriptions), paid out sick pay and death allowances, while the Benevolent Fund received ten shillings from each Sunday collection to 'give temporary assistance in money or goods or otherwise in cases of urgent necessity'. Two solicitors were prepared to give free legal advice to members who could not afford lawyers' fees. The Men's Society started a monthly magazine which, as noted, in 1907, became the church's magazine *Grafton News*.

The Cycling and Rambling Club was open to ladies and friends, and had more than 300 members. The Institute, which grew out of the minister's wish to create a club for ex-Boys' Brigade members, had rooms at the rear of the church in Grafton Square, with a reading room and a games room for billiards, chess, draughts and dominoes, together with cricket and football teams. These rooms were open each weeknight evening.

A Horticultural Society met monthly in Belmont Hall, which was also the venue for the weekly meeting of the Parliamentary Debating Society, which based its meetings on those of the House of Commons with 'all parties strongly represented'. The Men's Society arranged social meetings and smoking concerts during the winter, with excursions to the countryside and sports in the summer.

Dr Guinness Rogers had founded the Book Society in 1875. Its entry in the 1900 manual provides yet another an insight into the sociological make-up of the congregation.

> The Books will be changed by Messenger on alternate Monday mornings and sold after circulating 52 weeks. A Social Meeting (to which any member may introduce a Lady) will be held on the last Friday in October, November, January, February and March at the homes of members. As there are no fines, and the circuit is a very large one, the Members are ESPECIALLY REQUESTED to have the books ready for the Messenger when he calls, – and *when out of Town* to instruct their Servants to receive and give them back as usual, as any irregularity throws the whole circulation out of order.

The fact that this notice took it for granted that church members had servants reveals much about the class to which most church members belonged. Books discussed included: *Women of Shakespeare, The English Church in the Middle Ages, Use and Abuse of English, Bach, The Head as an Index of Race, Haircutting and Manicure* and *A Study in Psychology*.

In 1912 the church published an account of its work in a book entitled, *What we are doing at Grafton Square*. It contains chapters on various activities, with photographs of, for example, the Cycling Club.

There is also a description of the work undertaken at the Mission Hall on Wandsworth Road. A clinic was provided by a trained nurse, Sister Ella, who was particularly concerned with the care of mothers and babies. A photograph of the Women's Own club contains ranks of unsmiling women in dark clothes and large hats staring solemnly at the camera. This section ends with the words, 'Ladies, if you are free on Thursday afternoons, why not come and help at the Mission. You will have the consolation of doing good work and the women are so grateful.'

The 1915–16 church manual states that there were 55 babies on the baby clinic roll, with an average attendance of 25. Mothers received 'valuable assistance... in the rearing of their little ones'. Garments made by Sister Ella and a Mrs Stacey were able to be purchased from the clinic.

Clapham bore all the hallmarks of the 'Institutional Church' – a common approach to mission among Congregational churches in the nineteenth century. It was typical too of Free Church missions at the time, involving trying to fill all members' leisure time with religious and non-religious activity of an edifying nature.

This particular manual also provides an insight into how church life was affected by the Great War:

> All the organisations have suffered considerably owing to the strain of the War, and our Sunday Schools especially so, but notwithstanding the extra demand made on those at home in other ways, loyalty to the Schools has remained steadfast. Owing to difficulties with the railway company we could not have a joint Summer Excursion this year, so we divided the School into sections [each going its own way] ... This experiment proved highly satisfactory.

The Wandsworth Road Mission reported that attendance at Sunday school had dropped 'and this is due almost entirely to a reduced staff of teachers... four teachers are now serving in the Army or Navy and this is a heavy loss...'

The Girls Guild knitted scarves and mittens for soldiers and sailors and held a weekly collection to send parcels of chocolates or cigarettes 'to relatives of the girls on active service (chosen by ballot)'. Over 100 former members of the Boys' Brigade company had joined the Forces, and at least seven of these had been killed. The Boys' Brigade faced difficulties because five of its officers were also on active service.

The Mission's Thrift Club collected gifts of clothing and 'letters of introduction' to hospitals, surgical aid societies and convalescent homes. The Mothers' Meeting knitted socks, mittens, comforters etc. for the soldiers, while the church's Women's League sent parcels of clothing to Queen Mary's Needlework Guild and mattress covers to the soldiers' camp in Warminster.

The Men's Meeting suspended meetings for the duration of the war. The work of the Benevolent Society had been lightened by increased employment and military service, but income had diminished too and a collection from the Nine Elms branch of the Amalgamated Society of Locomotive Engineers and Firemen was gratefully acknowledged.

In October 1915 the church decided to set up a hostel for Belgian refugees and church member Mr H. G. Chalke placed a house in Lillieshall Road at the disposal of the church committee. Within four days, a party of eleven refugees had moved in, which included little children and a woman of 83. In February 1916 the hostel was moved to a larger house on Bedford Road, lent by an unnamed owner. Concerts were arranged for the residents; someone gave two tickets for the zoo and two parties visited Hampton Court. Each refugee was paid eight shillings a week for food and personal needs, while clothing, boot-repair and medical care were also provided. Two refugees were married at Easter 1916.

The manual's Roll of Honour now contained 125 names of men linked with the church or its organisations who were serving in the Forces. Of these, nine had been killed, and one had died in camp.

12

Some Graftonians

As noted the Minute Book of 1773 throws light on the sociological nature of the congregation as it went about choosing the minister, clerk, or pew-opener. The congregation had to subscribe at least two guineas per annum and trustees and managers of the church could only be drawn from those members subscribing a minimum of £25, and the annual rent for a whole pew was also £25. The guarantee of a seat required a yearly rent of £1. With no church meetings being held at that time, congregational life was based more on a business pattern rather than any ecclesiology.

Later in 1903, Dr Guinness Rogers noted in his autobiography that 'The Clapham church once had the reputation of being an extremely aristocratic community.' He spoke too of the mansions owned by Dissenters, who were people prominent in commerce, parliamentary and public life. The stipend he received speaks clearly of the wealth of his congregation.

Little has come to light regarding individual members but a study of the church's manual for 1903, 1906, 1908 and 1915–16, allied with the help of the internet, has turned up some information of interest. Details were found concerning some eminent families.

Colman

This was a branch of the Norwich mustard manufacturing family. Edward Colman was born in Clapham Common on 12 May 1808, the seventh son of Robert Colman of Rockland,

Norfolk. He was one of eleven brothers, who formed their own cricket team. In 1817 he married Eliza Fairley (1817–99) of Bow. He died in Clapham in 1874.

Jeremiah Colman JP was born in Clapham Common in 1853, the son of Edward Colman. In 1882 he married Annie, daughter of John Maple, of Bedford Lodge, Hampstead. He was Mayor of Hove (1899–1902), and of Queen Anne's Mansions, London SW1.

Stanley Colman was born in 1862 in Clapham Common and was the youngest son of Edward Colman. Another enthusiastic cricketer, he founded the (Clapham) Wanderers Cricket Club and was captain for over 50 years. He was also a player and a committee member at Surrey County Cricket Club. Stanley was a sprinter and played rugby for team of Clapham Rovers and also captained their football team. He died in 1942 in Walton-on-the-Hill.

Clement J. Colman was probably the most prominent member of this family in the life of the Clapham church. Clement was born at Montague House, Clapham, on 1 September 1851, the son of Edward and Eliza Colman. He was elected deacon in 1903 and played an active part in church life, as well as representing it on the London Congregational Union and Battersea & Clapham Free Church Council. He also attended the May meetings of the Congregational Union of England and Wales. With his main interest being church music, he was choirmaster for decades. His pride was his boys' choir – the only boys' choir in any Free Church in England. As has been noted, he produced *The Clapham Chant and Anthem Book* in 1886 (still available on Amazon). Colman became church treasurer in April 1906. Outside the church his passion, like his brothers, was cricket, being president of the Wanderers Cricket Club and a member of the Surrey County Cricket Club. He died on 19 May 1913.

Another son of Edward and Eliza was Frederick Edward Colman DL (London), who was born on 2 July 1841. In 1879 he married Helen (lady of the manors of North Tadworth, Preston and Burgh, eldest daughter of Davison Octavius Dalziel) and they had two sons. An industrialist, he was chairman of J. & J. Colman and a director of Reckitt & Colman. He lived in Nork Park, Epsom Downs, and Upper Grosvenor Street, London W1. He died 19 December 1899.

Colonel Frederick Gordon Dalziel Colman OBE TD was born on 25 March 1882 in Carlyle House, Chelsea Embankment, the son of Frederick Edward Colman DL and his wife Helen. He was baptised there privately by the Revd James Guinness Rogers in May 1882. He was educated at Eton. A passionate huntsman, he became Master of the Nork Hounds in 1904 at the age of 23, and the Belvoir Foxhounds in 1930. He bought Scalford Hall, Melton Mowbray, in 1944. He died in 1969.

Sir Nigel Claudian Dalziel Colman, 1st Baronet (1952), was born in Carlyle House, Chelsea Embankment, on 4 May 1886, the second son of Frederick Edward Colman DL and his wife. He too was baptised there privately by the Revd James Guinness Rogers and was educated at Eton. In 1952 he married Nona Ann Willan. Nigel was a director of Reckitt & Colman. An enthusiastic breeder and exhibitor of harness horses and dogs, he served as president of the National Horse Association of Great Britain (1939–45); president of the Hackney Horse Society in 1923 and 1938; chairman of the British Horse Society (1952–5); and received the medal of honour in 1953. He succeeded his uncle, Sir Davison Dalziel (Baron Dalziel of Wooller) as Conservative MP for Brixton (1927–45). He died at his Grosvenor Square home in March 1966.

Crace-Calvert

All Clapham members of the Crace-Calvert family were born in Australia. Dr George Alfred Crace-Calvert MB MRCS was born at Hobart, Tasmania, in 1871, the second son of William Frederick Crace-Calvert. After his education at Hutchins School, Hobart, he qualified as a physician at St Bartholomew's Medical School, London. In 1901 he married Ellen Marguerite, daughter of Francis Adams of Shamrock Lodge, Clapham Park, at Grafton Square. He was an Honorary Lieutenant of the church's Boys' Brigade. He lived in Clapham and Llanbedr Hall, Denbighshire, where he died in 1918.

Florence Elizabeth Crace-Calvert was born in Hobart in 1866 and was the daughter of Charles Crace-Calvert. Upon arriving in London she joined the Grafton Square church and was one of its representatives on the LMS Metropolitan Auxiliary Council. She returned to Australia with her sister Edith, and died at Turrmurra, New South Wales, in 1949.

Edith Catherine Crace-Calvert was born in Hobart in 1874, a daughter of Charles Crace-Calvert, and joined the church when she moved to Clapham. She died in New South Wales in 1941.

Glegg

Sir Alexander Glegg JP was born in Aberdeen in 1848, the son of Robert Glegg. He married Helen, daughter of William Robertson of Aberdeen and they had four children. Educated at the Gymnasium, Old Aberdeen, and Aberdeen University, he trained in marine engineering and worked in the design office of the Royal Arsenal, Woolwich, and then at printing engineers, R. Hole & Co. Glegg became chairman of linoleum manufacturers Barry & Staines, and a director of shipbuilders and engineers, Thorneycrofts Ltd. He is known for introducing aluminium as a medium for cooking food. A member of Wandsworth Borough Council, he served as Mayor of Wandsworth (1905–6). During the Great War he represented the Federation of Engineering Employers on the Women's Wages Arbitration Board, and was a member of the Metropolitan Munitions Board. He was elected deacon of the Clapham church in 1903 and represented them on the London Congregational Union and the Surrey Congregational Union. He was chairman of the British & Foreign Bible Society. Edward Lewis' departure from orthodox belief led to his resignation from the church in January 1907.

His death at his Wimbledon Park home in 1933 was reported in newspapers in many parts of the world.

Alexander Lindsay Glegg was born in 1900, the son of Sir Alexander Glegg. He was educated at London University, gaining a BSc in electrical engineering in 1903. After Glegg's conversion at the Keswick Convention in 1905 he became an evangelist, afterwards leading mission work in Wandsworth for more than 50 years. With Stuart Holden he founded the young people's meetings in Keswick in 1926 and the United Communion Service in 1929. A member of the Council of the Movement for World Evangelisation, he led the Royal Albert Hall mission in 1944. His death in 1993 received worldwide attention.

Grahame Robertson Glegg, the youngest son of Sir Alexander, was an engineer. With C. S. Macintyre he patented a device for giving change for paper money in 1928, and in the following year he patented his own improvements to change-giving apparatus. He was gazetted a captain in the 14th Battalion, County of London (London Scottish Regiment), after holding a similar rank in the Volunteer Force.

Kemp Welch

The Kemp Welch family had deep roots in Congregationalism. Martin Kemp (1723–72) was a ship-owner from Poole, Dorset, and co-founder of the Poole Town and Country Bank. In 1775 he married Mary, the daughter of Robert Welch of Lymington, and some time later Welch was added to the family name. Born into a local Congregationalist family, he was one of those expelled from the Hill Street Church, Poole, when it gained a Unitarian majority. Afterwards they worshipped for some time at Lag Lane, and then built a new chapel in Skinner Street, Poole. His son, Martin Kemp, a London merchant, was a resident of Clapham Common and a member of its Congregational Church, where he was followed by his son, Martin Kemp Welch, who, in turn, was succeeded by his son John.

John Kemp Welch (27 June 1810 – 1885) was born in Poole. He married Maria Cooper Rainsford and they had six sons and five daughters. A patent-starch manufacturer, he was chairman of Orlando Jones & Co. until his retirement in May 1883. With his partner William Evill, he purchased J. Schweppes & Co. on the death of Jacob Schweppes who had founded the mineral water company in Drury Lane, London. Under its new owners the company continued to sell its tonic water but added flavoured fizzy drinks. The company was appointed supplier of soda water to Queen Victoria in 1837. Schweppes became a limited company following the death of John Kemp Welch. In 1834 he purchased Sopley Park, a manor house on the edge of the New Forest, which he retained as his country dwelling. John Kemp Welch, a deacon at Clapham church, had a passionate interest in world mission, and served for many years as treasurer of the LMS. One of the society's missionaries in Papua, William Lawes (1839–1907), left Port Moresby in 1876 on an eastward expedition. He came to the river Wanigela, which he promptly renamed Kemp Welch, the name by which it has been known ever since. John Kemp Welch died in Christchurch, Dorset, on 21 January 1885.

Salt

Lady Caroline Salt was born in 1812 at the Manor House, Grimsby, the daughter of George Whitlam, a wealthy sheep farmer, and his wife Elizabeth. She was the youngest of eighteen children, of whom only eight survived. In 1830 she married Titus Salt (1803–76), who made regular visits to Lincolnshire to purchase wool for his family's company, D. Salt & Co., wool staplers of Bradford.

Later, Titus was to become a textile manufacturer, and then an alderman and second mayor of Bradford. He was its Liberal MP for two years and was a noted philanthropist, forever associated with his model village Saltaire. They had eleven children, five of whom predeceased their mother.

Mother and children all had Saltaire streets named after them. In 1869 Titus was created first baronet of Saltaire in the county of Yorkshire, and thus Caroline became Lady Salt. On the death of Sir Titus in 1876, Lady Salt sold their Crow Nest estate, near Halifax, and, accompanied by two unmarried daughters, Helen (1852–1924) and Ada (1853–1935), moved to Broadoak, a mansion overlooking Clapham Common. In 1883 Ada married Edmund Herbert Stevenson (1853–1918), a civil engineer from Streatham in Clapham. They were married by Dr Guinness Rogers. In 1893 Catherine died aged 81 at St Leonards where she had spent her summers. Guinness Rogers travelled to Saltaire to conduct her funeral. Broadoak was sold to the Xaverian Brothers, who opened a Catholic boys' school there in 1893.

After her mother's death Helen moved to Tunbridge Wells, where she was reunited with her sisters Amelia[1] and Ada. Her son, Herbert (1840–1912), did not enter the family business. Instead he became a gentleman farmer near Skipton. In the mid-1880s he sold up and moved to Brixton to marry Elizabeth Farrell (born 1854), a Roman Catholic 23 years his junior, in an Anglican church. He then became a Roman Catholic himself and was a keen parishioner of St Mary's, Clapham. Ten years later he moved to Clapham Common, South Side. Elizabeth died in 1889, aged 35, leaving four children. Ten years later Herbert married her widowed sister, Margaret de Lacey.

Searle

This was a family of prominent and prosperous architects. Charles Gray Searle (1818–81), the son of John Searle, stone merchant, was educated at Harrow. An architect and surveyor, he trained under Thomas Cubitt and set up his own business in 1846 at Paternoster House, London. After moving to Bloomsbury, he and his wife Kate left Kings Weigh House church and Congregationalism to join Bloomsbury Baptist Church. Some time in the late 1870s he moved to Clapham

Common with his wife and seven children and the family became connected once more with a Congregational church.

He was joined in business by his son, Septimus Cecil Searle (1853–1922), who gained his ARIBA in 1879. During his time in Clapham he was an officer of the Wandsworth Road Sunday school and became a deacon in 1903. Septimus was joined, in turn, by his son Norman Odell Searle ARIBA (1881–?), who at the age of 25 became a partner in Searle & Searle. Norman Odell Searle, an officer in the Boys' Brigade, joined the army in the Great War with a commission.

Norman's brother Gilbert Odell Searle, also a Boys' Brigade officer, chose not to enter the family business. Educated at Dulwich College, he gained a BSc at Wye College in agricultural science. In 1914 he was commissioned in the army, rising to the rank of major. The end of hostilities saw him return to college, this time in Cambridge, prior to his joining the staff of the Linen Industry Research Establishment in Northern Ireland. In the 1940s he was superintendent of HM Norfolk Flax Establishment in Flitcham Abbey, Norfolk.

Alice Benham

The Clapham congregation included a number of medical practitioners in a local practice with some venturing farther afield. Dr Alice Benham gained her MB degree in 1904 and her MD in 1910, both from London University. She became medical officer at the Church Army Dispensary, London. In 1914 she joined the Millicent Fawcett hospital units, under the British Red Cross, founded by Dame Millicent Garrett Fawcett, president of the National Union of Women's Suffrage Societies (NUWSS), becoming a member of its committee. That year she was posted to the British field hospital in Antwerp. In December 1915 the NUWSS appealed to friends and supporters for funds to help sick and homeless refugee women in Russia. Alice Benham was one of those who went to Russia in 1915. Based at the hospital at Stara Chelnoe, on a tributary of the

Volga, a district without a doctor, she treated both refugees and peasants until her return to London in 1916. On 18 September 1921 she was quoted in the Australian newspaper, *The Perth Sunday Times*, as favouring women's football teams, though living in London at the time.

George Arthur Farmiloe

Arthur Farmiloe was the son of William Farmiloe (1827–97) of 15 Cedars Road, Clapham, and Amelia Waters (1822–?). His first wife died 1907 and in 1909 he married Constance Eveline (1877–1938), daughter of Willem Boissevain and Cecilia Henrietta Catherine Nugent, from Amsterdam. He was a director of Arthur Farmiloe & Co., stained glass and paint manufacturers. At Grafton Square he was treasurer of the Wandsworth Road Mission Sunday school. He lived in Mayfair, then at Rochester Row, Westminster.

W. Martin Smith

Martin Smith is representative of those Clapham members involved in the life of the wider church. A wharfmonger and chairman of W. M. Smith & Sons, he was elected chairman of the Wharfmongers Association. Elected deacon in 1862, he became superintendent of the Belmont Road Sunday school in the same year and was elected church treasurer in 1903. Smith served as chairman and treasurer of Hackney College for sixteen years. He was treasurer of the Surrey Congregational Union for 33 years until elected chairman, and thereafter resumed the role of treasurer until his death. He also represented the church on the London Congregational Union. He too resigned from the church in 1907 because of Edward Lewis' doctrinal standpoint. Smith died in November 1907.

W. W. Beare

In addition to John Kemp-Smith, at least one member served as a director of the LMS. W. W. Beare was also treasurer of the

London Metropolitan Auxiliary. He was a liberal subscriber to the work in China and Papua. Born in Walworth in 1820, he became a member of the Congregational church there. When he retired from business at an early age, he built a house in Atkins Road, Clapham Park. He joined the church in Clapham, where he was later elected deacon. He acted as treasurer of the church's book society as well as treasurer and administrator of the Communion fund. Beare died at his Tenby home in May 1902.

Richard Lovett

Clapham held an attraction for ministers not in pastoral charge. Among them was the Revd Richard Lovett MA. Lovett was born in Croydon in 1851, the son of Richard Deacon Lovett and Annie Godart. In 1879 he married Annie Hancock, daughter of William Reynolds of Lowood, Torquay. Educated at Cheshunt College, he gained a BA in philosophy from London University in 1873, and his Master's degree one year later. Lovett was an assistant master at Bishop's Stortford College (1874–6), and then became minister of St Stephen's Countess of Huntingdon's Connexion, Rochdale (1876–82). He joined the Religious Tract Society as its editor (1891–1900) and then secretary (1900–40). He became a deacon at Clapham in 1903. Lovett died on 22 December 1904. He published *Norwegian Pictures, drawn with pen and pencil* (1885); *London Pictures Drawn with Pen and Pencil* (1890); *London 100 Years Ago* (1890); *United States Pictures* (1891); *The Charm of Victorian London Illustrated* (1890); *James Gilmour of Mongolia* (1892); *The History of the London Missionary Society, 1795–1895* (1899); *The English Bible in the John Rylands Library* (1899); *James Chalmers his Autobiography and Letters* (1902).

His son, Frederick Reynolds Lovett MA, became a deacon in 1915. He represented the church on the LMS Metropolitan Auxiliary and was secretary and treasurer of the church's hostel for Belgian refugees during the Great War. He wrote the church history in 1912.

Paul James Turquand

The Revd Paul James Turquand was born in Milford, Hampshire, in 1826, the son of a Baptist minister of Huguenot descent. He was educated at Fakenham Preparatory Academy, Homerton Academy and New College, Oxford. Ordained in 1853, he became co-pastor of York Street, Walworth (1853–5); then sole pastor (1855–93). He retired to Clapham in 1894. He was secretary of the Surrey Congregational Union (1880–1902), resigning shortly after the death of his wife. He was also secretary of the Congregational Fund Board (1885–1901) and a member of the deputation of the three dissenting bodies to Queen Victoria, 1898. He died suddenly while reading in his study chair on 12 August 1902.

Stanley Melville Wright

The church contained a sprinkling of both branches of the legal profession, including prominent solicitors based in the City. Stanley M. Wright was one of those people who were allowed to retain their church membership while living abroad. Wright was a barrister living in Jubbulpore, India. He died in Bombay following what was believed to have been a snake or insect bite.

E. H. Highton

Several members were pioneers in their own fields. E. H. Highton, an early motoring enthusiast, was chairman of the English Automobile Horseless Carriage Syndicate Ltd until it was wound up in 1897. He became a deacon in Clapham at 1903, and was also a representative to the Surrey Congregational Union. Highton was one of the five deacons who left the church in 1907 in protest at the doctrine preached by Edward Lewis.

Albert Knight Croad

Albert Knight Croad was elected an associate of the Royal Aeronautical Society in 1920. He married Marta Louise Otto, a

German lady. Their son, born in 1891, was educated at Melton Mowbray Grammar School; Worcester College and Royal Technical College, Glasgow, where he graduated in chemistry. He then proceeded to Leipzig University, but was interned in Germany at the outbreak of war in 1914.

Sidney Herbert Wells

Sidney Herbert Wells CBE AMICE was born in Cottenham, Cambridgeshire, on 10 August 1865, the son of the Revd J. C. Wells, a Baptist minister. He married firstly in 1890 to Mary Elizabeth (died 1907), daughter of George Mathew, Worsted Hall, Cambridge. They had two daughters. In 1908 he married his sister-in-law, Florence Amelia Matthew. Wells was educated at Whitworth School and Birbeck College and King's College, London, gaining a BSc in engineering. He was a founder of the Institute of Junior Engineers in 1889 and its chairman for five sessions. After working as a master at Dulwich College (1889–91), he became a senior assistant in the Engineering department of Leeds University (1891–3), prior to his appointment as the first principal of Battersea College (1893–1907). An original member of the Faculty of Engineering at London University, he was secretary of the Board of Studies (1903–5) and of the faculty in 1905. He served on the Incorporated Council of the Association of Technical Institutions in 1894 and as its Honourable Secretary (1903–7). Wells was a member of the examinations board of the City & Guilds Institute (1903), the Teachers' Registration Council (1904), and the consultative committee of the Board of Education (1904). He visited Egypt to report on technical education in 1906. In 1907 he was appointed director general of the Department of Commercial Education in Cairo, and was awarded the Order of Medjidieh (2nd Class) and the Order of the Nile (2nd Class), as well as being mentioned in General Allenby's dispatches. Wells was vice-chairman of the Egyptian Commission of Commerce and Industry (1916–18), and director of Civilian Employment for EEF (1917–19). He died in St Leonards in 1923.

Organists

The choral tradition at Grafton Square necessitated the appointment of organists of note. Details of two of these have come to hand.

John Post Attwater Mus. Bac. LRCO LRAM JP was born in Faversham in 1862 and died in Clapham in 1909. An organ pupil of Dr Charles Joseph Frost, he taught at Battersea Polytechnic. Three of his organ works are still available: *Hommage a Handel 76/3*; *Larghetto Op. 76/2* and *Scherzo Op. 76/1*.

Dr Francis W. Sutton BMus FRCO, a native of Borough, London, was a student at the Guildhall School of Music and an assistant organist at St John's, London Bridge, and then at Southwark cathedral (1917–22). An organist at several London churches, the Middlesex Hospital and the BBC, at least one of his works is obtainable today: *Twenty-four complete sets of exercises in sight-reading (with pedals), transposition (with pedals), score-reading (without pedals), [and] hymn-tune harmonisation (with pedals): similar to tests set for examinations in organ playing (F.R.C.O., etc.).*

Members of Parliament

Clapham was a popular residential area for Members of Parliament and a number worshipped regularly or from time to time at Grafton Square, especially during the ministry of Dr Guinness Rogers, possibly as much for his politics as for his preaching.

William Sproston Caine JP (1842–1903) was born in Seacombe, Cheshire, the son of Nathaniel Caine, a metal merchant. He married Alice, daughter of the Revd Hugh Stowell Brown. After leaving Birkenhead School, he entered his father's business, becoming a partner in 1864. He gained control of Shaw's Brown Iron Company, Liverpool, in 1878, leaving the running of his inherited business to his partner and that business collapsed in 1893 – the debts were cleared but his resources thereafter were used to clear the mortgage he raised to pay off the debts.

Caine was a member of a Baptist church in Liverpool and then of Stockwell Baptist Church. A zealous temperance reformer, he served as chairman of the Popular Control and Licence Reform Association and vice-president of the temperance movement, United Kingdom Alliance. He was also president of the Baptist Total Abstinence Society, the Congregational Temperance Society, the British Temperance League and the National Temperance Federation, and secretary of the Anglo-Indian Temperance Association.

It was the temperance cause which led him into active politics and he became Liberal MP for Scarborough (1880–5). Elected as Liberal Unionist MP for Barrow-in-Furness (1886–90), he took an active part in forming this new party and became its Chief Whip. His temperance views clashed with those of his Conservative allies. He resigned his seat and position as Chief Whip in protest against the Government's neglect of Irish local government and for adopting compensation payments for publicans. He unsuccessfully fought the ensuing by-election as an Independent Liberal. He returned to the Liberal Party and served as MP for Bradford East (1892–5); and for Cornwall North-West (Camborne), 1900–3. He was Civil Lord of the Admiralty (1884–5). Caine was a member of the Royal Commission on Licensing Laws, and that on Indian finance. This Liberal MP who lived in North Side, Clapham, had some links with the church, though a Baptist, as his second daughter, Dorothea Caine MD, was married there on 16 November 1898, to Walter Stacey Colman MD FRCP (1864–1932), son of Samuel C. Colman (of the Peterborough branch of the family). His daughter Ruth was married also at the church, in 1897, to J. Herbert Lewis MP Lady Ruth Herbert Lewis became an authority on Welsh folk songs, and she was honoured for her work with the creation of the Lady Herbert Lewis Memorial Competition, the chief competition for individual folk singers at the National Eisteddfod of Wales.

Sir Herbert Hardy Cozens-Hardy, 1st Baron Cozens-Hardy of Letheringsett (1914) QC (1838–1920) was born in

Letheringsett Hall, Holt, Norfolk, the second son of W. H. Cozens-Hardy JP. His sister married Jeremiah James Colman. Cozens-Hardy was married at Grafton Square in 1866 to Maria (died 1886), who was daughter of Thomas Hepburn of Clapham Common, a wealthy leather merchant. They had two sons and two daughters. He was educated at Amersham School and studied law at University College London. He was elected Fellow of University College London and called to the Bar in 1862, becoming a Bencher of Lincoln's Inn. He served as Liberal MP for North Norfolk (1885–February 1899). He was chairman of the General Council of the Bar (1899). Knighted on becoming a High Court Judge in 1889, he was appointed Lord Justice of Appeal and a member of the Privy Council in 1901. He served as Master of the Rolls (1907–18).

Cozens-Hardy was brought up Wesleyan, but his parents became Free Methodists. He was a member of Bloomsbury Baptist Church from 1856. During his period as an MP he transferred his membership to Whitefield's Tabernacle Congregational Church. He lived in Ladbroke Grove, London, and Letheringsett Hall, Holt, Norfolk.

Sir Henry Jackson, 1st Baronet, MA BSc MB JP (22 August 1875 – 23 February 1937), was a scientist and physician. Born in Heywood, Lancashire, in 1875, he was the son of James and Sarah Jackson. In 1904 he married Edith Margaret, daughter of Joseph Stanley of Norton Grange, Castleton. Jackson was educated at Bury Grammar School and studied natural science at Downing College, Cambridge. There then followed spells at London University and Edinburgh University. He was a Fellow and tutor at Downing College (1901–11), a Fellow of the Cambridge Philosophical Society and a Fellow of the Federation of Medical and Applied Sciences.

A general practitioner, he served as a major in the Royal Army Medical Corps during the Great War. Elected to Wandsworth Borough Council, he was mayor of the borough (1921–4). He acted as chairman of the Metropolitan Boroughs Standing Joint Committee (1924), the Greater London Joint Smoke

Abatement Committee, and the London and Home Counties Advisory Committee on Traffic (1933), as well as being a trustee of the London Passenger Transport Board. He was also treasurer of Bolingbroke Hospital, Wandsworth Common, and president of London University Conservative Association.

In 1924 he was elected Member of Parliament for Wandsworth Central, but was narrowly defeated at the 1929 general election by the Labour Party candidate, Archibald George Church. At the next election in 1931, Church did not stand again, and Jackson took the seat with a large majority. He was re-elected in 1935, and held the seat until his death. In the House of Commons, he was chairman of the Standing Committee on Mineral Transport (1932), and of the Conservative Parliamentary Transport Committee. Henry Jackson collapsed as he was finishing his address at a London dinner in February 1937. He'd been knighted on 1 March 1924, and made a baronet on 4 July 1935 for services in connection with transport questions. The title became extinct at his death.

***

One name has come to light which stands out because it reveals a greater social mix at the church than the other names might have suggested. Mabel Ruddenham was born in Brixton in 1893, one of the six children of Robert J. Ruddenham (born Norfolk 1866), a stonemason's labourer. Mabel became a ledger clerk, as did her sisters Gertrude and Mabel, while one brother Edwin Robert was apprenticed to a printer before joining the navy and was lost at sea in September 1914.

13

Into all the World

THE CLAPHAM CHURCH showed a strong interest in overseas mission, as is borne out by its collections for the LMS. In 1903 these came to £639-3-9; £364-16-11 (1906); £343-13-2 (1908); £207-3-8 (1914) and £150-17-7 (1915). The 1903 figures include £140-3-7 contributed to the LMS Deficiency Fund and £100 to honour the work of Dr Griffith John.[1] The involvement of church members in the home organisation of the LMS has already been noted. The decline shown in the 1914–15 amounts can be explained, in part, by the opening of the church's hostel for Belgian refugees, to which £295-7-6 was donated in the eight months following October 1914. A clause concerning the roll of membership in the church rules reads: 'In the case of members (other than missionary members) who leave the district without making application for transfer, their names shall lapse after twelve months, unless special circumstances justify the retention of their names.'

At least nine church members served overseas under the auspices of the LMS in the period between 1860 and 1914.

The Revd James Wilberforce Sibree has been named, and is listed on the membership roll for 1915 as being in Leulumoega, Upolu, Samoa. All his siblings too followed their parents to the mission field. His sister, Dr Alice Sibree, was for some time a member of the Clapham church. She was born at Antanarivo, Madagascar, in 1876. Educated at the London School of Medicine for Women, she gained her MB and LRCP and then proceeded in 1904 to Hong Kong to work as an obstetrician in its first maternity hospital (later give the name 'Alice Memorial'). Disagreement with the medical superintendent led to her resignation in 1909, followed by her return to Britain, where she undertook deputation work for the LMS. Later she returned to Hong Kong as a volunteer medical mission worker and married H. H. Hickling, manager of the Tikoo Sugar Refinery. Alice Sibree was the driving force in founding the Tsan Yuk Hospital in 1922. She was awarded the MBE and became a Sister of the Order of Saint John of Jerusalem.

The Revd George Sydney Owen was born in Pembroke on 2 January 1843 and educated at Bedford and Highgate academies. Ordained in 1861, he served as an LMS missionary in China (1865–72) before accepting an appointment with the Japanese government in Tokyo in 1872. He returned to Peking (Beijing) to work for the LMS (1875–1902). From 1908 to 1913 he was professor of Chinese at King's College, London, and undertook the revision of the Bible in Mandarin (the Chinese Union version, considered by many to be the Chinese Protestant's Bible), 1902–6. During their time in London he and his wife lived in Morella Road, Wandsworth Common, and George became a church member in Grafton Square, though Mrs Owen is not listed in the 1915 church roll. George Owen died on 8 February 1914.

The Revd Charles Frederick Moss was born in Holbeach, Lincolnshire, in 1835. After training for the ministry in New College, London, he served pastorates in Gosport, Hampshire (1862–7) and Torrington (1867–70). In 1870 the LMS appointed him to serve in Madagascar, where he remained until 1882. From 1884 to 1899 he was minister at Birkdale, Lancashire, and then became an agent with the British and Foreign Bible Society. He and his wife were members at Clapham. He died on 24 May 1894.

The Revd Henry Theophilus Johnson was born in Plymouth on 24 November 1855, and was educated at Cheshunt College. He was ordained in May 1881 and married Henrietta Kate Widger shortly afterwards. He and Kate were missionaries in

Betsileio, Madagascar, from 1881 to 1919. He acted as temporary principal of the theological seminary in 1891. Johnson then undertook deputation work for the LMS (1919–21). He was elected an honorary deacon at Clapham in 1928. He died 18 March 1939, followed by Kate on 26 February 1941.

The Revd Edwin Pryce Jones was born on 1 June 1864 in Aberdeen. He trained for the ministry at Hackney College and was appointed to Farafangana in south-east Madagascar. He was ordained 15 March 1893 and married Minnie Ellis Page fifteen days later. They sailed from Britain on 26 May 1893 and arrived in Manajara on 6 July and went on to Farafangana where they settled. After the French conquest of the island the Farafangana mission was handed over to the Norwegian Mission. Mr and Mrs Jones then returned to Britain, arriving on 10 July 1898. He was appointed to the Papua mission and they left Britain once more on 28 April 1899 to work in Jokea, Papua. His Papuan name was Sioni of Moru. In 1915, they went to Australia for deputation work. Edwin Pryce Jones died on 27 July 1928. He was listed as an associate member in Clapham.

Dr Cheng Jingyi (1881–1940) was born in Beijing, the son of a pastor with the LMS. After studying the Chinese Classics, he entered the LMS Anglo-Chinese College in Beijing and then proceeded to the Society's theological college at Tienstin (Tianjan), from where he graduated in 1900. Two weeks later he and his family were caught up in the Boxer Rebellion,[2] during which they escaped death on six occasions before finding refuge at the British legation, where they endured great privation. During this period a young sister died and his two younger brothers suffered permanent injury. All of this greatly impacted on the young Chinese Christian who came to London to assist George Owen in his Bible translating work and joined the Clapham church. He resigned his church membership in September 1906 and then travelled to Glasgow to spend two years at its Bible training institute. In the summer of 1908 he returned to China and served as an assistant pastor at the Mi-shi Hutong Church in Beijing, whose membership included a number of Chinese professional people and academics. He returned to Scotland for the 1910 Edinburgh Missionary Conference and distinguished himself by presenting what has been called its best speech. In his remarks he said:

> As a representative of the Chinese Church, I speak entirely from the Chinese standpoint... Speaking plainly we hope to see, in the near future, a united Christian Church without any denominational distinctions. This may seem somewhat peculiar to you, but, friends, do not forget to view us from our standpoint, and if you fail to do that, the Chinese will remain always as a mysterious people to you.

After returning to Beijing, he was ordained as pastor of the Mi-shi Hutong Church which, though associated with the LMS, was an independent Chinese church. Cheng took a prominent role in promoting indigenous Christianity in China. This movement had begun in the mid-nineteenth century with the 'three-self' movements initiated by missionaries. This included the development of the First and Second Amoy Church in Xiamen, as well as the self-governing presbyteries under the English Presbyterian mission in Swatow. It was influenced too by the indigenous movements started by local Chinese Christians in response to the Boxer Rebellion.

In 1917 he led a campaign against a government plan to allow only Confucian moral instruction in schools. He founded the China for Christ movement in 1919 and helped found the indigenous interdenominational Chinese Home Mission Society to reach ethnic groups in south-west China. He was general secretary of the National Christian Council from its establishment in 1922 until his resignation in 1933 due to poor health. In 1927 Cheng was elected the first moderator of the Church of Christ in China, a Protestant ecumenical organization comprising sixteen denominations. He was on the executive committee of the International Missionary Conference from

1928 to 1938 and was awarded honorary doctorates from Knox College, Toronto, Canada (1916); the College of Wooster, Ohio, USA (1923); and St John's University, Shanghai (1929). He died in Shanghai after his visit to the mission in south-west China and Guizhou in 1939.

14

Strength and Weakness

ANOTHER TWO YEARS elapsed before Edward Lewis was succeeded in 1911 by the Revd William Morton Barwell MA, the son of Congregational minister William Barwell. He was born in Cheltenham on 26 April 1875, and educated at Cheltenham schools. After working as a draper's assistant in Cheltenham and Liverpool, he trained for the ministry at Mansfield College, Oxford. When he was a student-pastor in Woburn, Bedfordshire, he wrote *A Short History of Woburn Congregational Church*. In 1901 he was ordained at Morningside Congregational Church, Edinburgh, where he ministered until his move to Clapham.

The *Clapham Observer* published a long and detailed account of the 'Interesting Recognition Service at Grafton Square' at Barwell's induction. Among the many speakers was the Revd C. Silvester Horne MP, chairman of the Congregational Union of England and Wales, who gave the main address. The Revd W. B. Selbie, principal of Barwell's alma mater, Mansfield College, Oxford, declared that the church could not have called:

> … a man better able than Mr Barwell to serve them, not only with straightforwardness and courage, but also with deep and large-hearted sympathy, culture and enthusiasm, and to be in every way the man they had wanted and waited for – and one whom he joined most heartily in thanking God for having sent there (applause).

Revd William Morton Bartwell

Mr H. Brown, representing the Morningside Church, said:

... that that gentleman's one fault was a desire to do what was more than human strength permitted. Mr Barwell was full of youth, energy and the old desire to spend and be spent in the service of the Church. Therefore, he hoped they would be kind to him at Grafton Square (applause).

The former minister, Edward W. Lewis, in his words of welcome, pointed out to the congregation that:

Mr Barwell's pastorate, however, would largely depend on his people and, if his ministry had been moulded in the north it must not be marred in the south. In the north they had surrounded Mr Barwell with everything that would make a ministry enjoyable and profitable. Then he took it that Clapham, at any rate, did not mean to be outdone in hospitality by Edinburgh, but meant to give him the sunniest and most summery time of his life (applause).

The service was chaired by Clement Colman, the church treasurer. In outlining the history of the call, his statement that the church meeting held on 29 December 1910 had issued a unanimous call was greeted with applause. Colman added:

What struck us was not only his powers as a preacher with original and fresh thoughts, but the intense spirituality with which he conducted the services... We believe that there is an opening in London, and especially in this church, for a man of Mr Barwell's qualifications and it may be some slight consolation to our Scotch friends to know that he will receive our wholehearted support, and we shall leave nothing undone to show our affection for him and, as a consequence, compel him to have a tender regard for us.

Sadly, this is not how the situation worked itself out. According to John Drennan in the 1960s:

> He was a very different man from his predecessor in appearance and style. He was a sincere and kindly man, but his preaching was not of a quality to attract the fickle London congregations. Clapham too had changed. Many of the big houses were now broken up into flats, and flat dwellers come and go, and are not regular church goers. As the church began to decline, attendances fell away, and money problems became pressing. The outbreak of the Great War in 1914 created fresh problems... On the advice of the deacons, a strong-minded body of men, Mr Barwell left for another pastorate.

Barwell's later pastorates were at Victoria Road, Harrogate (1913–26); Trinity Church, St Albans (1926–44) and Headgate Church, Colchester (1944–9). He was a director of the LMS for 40 years, and its chairman in 1936. As was to happen again in the early 1930s, a good minister followed one who possessed a powerful, charismatic personality, the memory of whom made the work and life of his successor doomed to failure. A gifted man, Barwell appears to have lacked the toughness needed to control and guide the Clapham deacons, who treated him badly, as they did the next minister but one.

Morton Barwell has been profiled as a remarkable and saintly man by some. His letter accepting the call to Clapham in 1911 expresses gratitude for the stipend he was to receive but said that he would prefer to take £200 less per annum rather than support some of the methods used to raise the necessary funds. His offer was not accepted. His obituary in the *Congregational Year Book* describes him as:

> ... a fine preacher, a loving pastor, a pacifist and a reconciler... He learned German in order to preach and lecture to German prisoners-of-war... One of our very best ministers... He knew much

personal trouble but by faith and prayer he turned all his sorrows into strength and returned all injuries with blessings. He was a great exponent and exampler of the Christian faith. Many would say that he was the most Christ-like man they had ever known, that they never knew him to do a selfish thing or say an unkind word.

He died in his vestry in Colchester after morning service on 31 October 1949.

One important event during Barwell's pastorate was a commemoration held between 29 September and 6 October 1912 to celebrate the 250th anniversary of the Great Ejectment in 1662 and the diamond jubilee of the opening of the Grafton Square building on 29 September 1852. One of the important events of the week was the unveiling of a memorial window to Dr J. Guinness Rogers. The Revd Dr John Hunter of Glasgow was the guest preacher on that Sunday. Among the speakers who took part in meetings during the week were Sir Albert Spicer Bt., MP for Central Hackney, the first lay chairman of the Congregational Union of England and Wales (1893) and a former treasurer of the LMS, a cause dear to the heart of the Clapham church; the Revd Dr J. D. Jones of Bournemouth; Dr Rowland; the Revd C. Silvester Horne MP; the Revd Bernard Snell of Brixton and the former pastor, Edward W. Lewis. *A History of Clapham Congregational Church* by F. Reynolds Lovett was published, as was another book, *What We Are Doing at Grafton Square.*

***

In 1915 a tougher character arrived in the person of George Stanley Russell MA BD. One cannot tell whether Russell was aware of the rough treatment handed out to his predecessor by the Clapham deacons, but in a letter published in the church manual prior to his arrival the minister-elect declared:

> I have always possessed from my churches, since the day of my Ordination, a freedom of speech and action which has been – from

my temperament – an indispensable condition of success. None of those churches has ever regretted the untrammelled liberty of which they made me the steward. The ministry which is hedged in by convention, formality and tradition and in which, instead of being the servant of all, a man becomes the hireling of each, is to me so repugnant that I could not have entered it and should not remain in it.

Clearly a very different personality from his predecessor. He stated too that he intended to concentrate on preaching 'a lively and virile message' and on bringing 'to the services of the Sanctuary an added beauty and dignity, while preserving their simplicity'.

The new minister was born in Great Grimsby in March 1883, the son of Joseph Russell, deacon and Sunday school superintendent at Spring Church in the town, and Isabella Wells Forbes. He was educated at Aberdeen Grammar and Aberdeen University, where he read psychology. He left the United Free Church of Scotland to become a Congregationalist, though many of his writings suggest that, at heart, he remained a Presbyterian. After training for the ministry at the Yorkshire United College, Bradford, he was ordained in 1907 and served Hopton Congregational Church, Mirfield (1909–11), and St-Annes-on-Sea, Lancashire (1911–15). In 1913 he married Ethel, daughter of D. M. Tait of Toronto, Canada.

Russell robed the choir of 24 boys and twelve men in cassock and surplice, with the boys also wearing ruffles (seemingly at first to hide the grubby collars of some of the boys).[1] Later women were added to the choir (without hats). Liturgical forms of worship were introduced:

> ... in which the beautiful prayers of the Church of England were prominent... we had a musical standard unequalled by any Nonconformist church I knew, sufficiently high for Dr Vaughan Williams to come and sing on occasions, under my organist... [it] brought many Anglicans into membership because their own churches were too 'low'.[2]

Russell's name has been linked with *A Free Church Book of Common Prayer*, published in 1929. The worship patterns he introduced at Clapham were further developed by him later in Canada, culminating in his publishing his *A Book of Public Worship*.[3] Many new musical societies were formed and old ones revived: the dramatic society performed Shakespeare twice a year, directed by the minister, who always played the main male part!

One member of the large Sunday congregations at this time was Pamela Hansford Johnson,[4] a novelist, playwright, poet, literary and social critic. Her civil servant father spent most of his life in West Africa, while she and her mother lived in Battersea Rise. She accompanied her mother to morning worship at St Mark's, Battersea Rise, where she came to enjoy the ritual. Then, when she was fifteen, an aunt insisted that she go with her to the Congregational church in Grafton Square.

Johnson recalled Stanley Russell's fine voice and love of ritual. Worship there was like that at no other Congregational church, with its liturgical forms and wonderful music. Russell's extempore prayers appealed to her, as did his practice of baptising children at morning worship in the presence of the whole congregation. Though the sermons could be rather long, they were good, often with texts from Shakespeare or George Bernard Shaw. Most of Clapham's intellectuals, of whom there were many, were attracted to the church, as was a sizeable gay representation. Societies flourished and among guest performers were the young John Barbirolli and William Primrose. Pamela Hansford Johnson became a church member but after Russell's departure she eventually returned to Anglicanism.

It was during his time in Clapham that Russell became a pacifist. He records in the moving chapter entitled 'Into the War and Out of It' in his autobiography that his attempts to join the army at the outbreak of the Great War failed on medical grounds, when he was described as 'For Garrison and Hospital duty at home'. He remained a minister in Clapham therefore, but also obtained an appointment as chaplain (with the honorary rank of Captain) to the 2,500-bed King George Hospital, Stamford Street (1915–19), and to the Tower of London (1914–19). The suffering of the young men he met at the hospital brought about a profound change:

> The Great War, and especially the crucifixion of youth by cynicism, greed and cruelty, which formed its leading feature, made me a pacifist... No one seems to realize that a boy of eighteen is, for all his show of manhood, about the most delicately fashioned mechanism on earth, and that, to subject him to the callous attitudes of wartime is an abomination beyond description.[5]

He continued his ministry after the war as chaplain to Queen Alexandra's Home for Paralysed Soldiers (1919–29). The Clapham minister became a member of the International Christian Council (British Section), 'the object of which was to bring the pressure of Christian opinion on both sides to stop or at least to mitigate the horrors of war.'[6] After the war he served on the national committee of the No Conscription Union. In addition he was president of the Congregational Ministers' Crusade Against War (1927–9).

Stanley Russell was prominent in the life of the community living around Clapham Common. A Rotarian, he was a founder member of the Clapham Rotary Club and later its president. The club presented him with an inscribed fountain pen when he later departed for Canada. He was a personal friend of Prime Minister H. H. Asquith from the time when, as a student, he organised Asquith's unsuccessful election campaign for the Rectorship of Aberdeen University. During his time in Clapham, Russell was elected president of the local division of the Liberal Association. Though, when church member, Sir Henry Jackson, Conservative MP for Central Wandsworth lost his seat in 1929, Russell appeared to share his distress in a letter written to another church member. (Jackson was re-elected in 1931 but died while delivering a speech in 1938.)

Revd G. Stanley Russell

Russell was involved in wider denominational affairs too, serving as a very active chairman of the London Congregational Union (1928–9): 'I was head of his [Lord Mayor of London] religious denomination for an area covering ten miles from Charing Cross and containing some 250 churches of our order.'[7] Previously he had chaired its Central Home Mission committee (1923–9). He was a member also of the council of the Congregational Union of England and Wales and took a prominent role in talks with the Presbyterian Church of England, addressing the ministers of its London Presbytery on the subject.

According to John Drennan:

Mr Russell was a big, handsome, dark man with plenty of energy and initiative. As a preacher he was outstanding, eloquent and oratorically dramatic. He was a great reader and his sermons were embellished with quotations from many sources. He could make a forty-minute sermon seem short. His sermons each month on some new book were especially popular. Church attendances revived remarkably and people came long distances to hear him. It is true that many of these were 'sermon tasters' who came for entertainment rather than for conviction, but there were many who joined the church... Mr Russell was particularly successful in managing his deacons who were a tough lot. Under his chairmanship they became an excellent team and for many years all went well.

Russell controlled them so well that he was able to spend three summer months at a Canadian church on alternate summers.

A celebration was held at Belmont Hall on 24 September 1925 to mark a triple anniversary: the founding of the church which, according to a report in next day's *Clapham Observer* was 'the fourth of its denomination in the country'; the 73rd anniversary of the opening of the Grafton Square chapel; and the tenth anniversary of the minister's induction. The local newspaper announced 'Congratulations from State, Church and Stage'. Letters were read from his old friend and former Liberal Prime Minister, H. H. Asquith, now the Earl of Oxford and Asquith; actress Phyllis Neilson-Terry, and the Dean of Durham, as well as from a host of well-known Congregational ministers. Among the speakers were church secretary F. J. Ware, church member Sir James Carmichael KBE, Conservative MP Sir Henry Jackson Bt., the Revd Thomas Yates, former Chairman of the Congregational Union of England and Wales and also the Revd W. E. Orchard.

It should have been no surprise therefore to hear that eventually Russell wished to move to Canada permanently. It was known that he had refused calls to Canada and Edinburgh and, just a few months earlier, the deacons had persuaded him not to move to Brighton as a successor to Dr T. Rhondda Williams. So the news that the minister expected a call from Deer Park Presbyterian Church, Toronto, came as a bombshell to the Clapham deacons. Minutes of the deacons' meeting at the time show these tough city gents virtually grovelling in their attempts to persuade Russell not to leave. A draft letter of three-and-a-half typed pages, dated 1 June 1929, in reply to Russell's letter said:

> There must have been some ups and downs in the course of the years and we recognise that there have been troublesome personal matters in the last few months. We also recognise that your term of office as Chairman of the London Congregational Union made large demands on your strength and energy. But we do plead that these passing troubles should not sway your judgement in coming to a decision of such importance as that of laying down your work here.[8]

The plea fell on deaf ears. He was ready to move after fourteen years in Clapham, 'not the least strenuous of spheres and I feel that my work here is done.'[9]

On 5 June he wrote formally to the church secretary informing him that he had 'received by cable a unanimous and enthusiastic invitation to the pastorate of Deer Park United Church, Toronto. I cabled them in reply that I shall make my decision by Sunday.' The next day he sent his letter of resignation to the church secretary, together with a personal letter in which he wrote:

> The idea that there is any contribution made to my decision by disturbances of a personal character is absolutely without foundation, nor must the onus be laid on my Chairmanship of the London Congregational Union – strenuous as that was. It is to be set down to the fact that, both in the pulpit and elsewhere (perhaps especially the latter) Grafton Square is a very exacting pastorate... I shall be surprised and sorry that [my] work was so superficial that – with the enthusiastic and united leadership of an unusually vigorous diaconate – it just crumbles.

A handwritten postscript to a further letter to the church secretary on 14 June tells that Russell has newly received a copy of the Deer Park Year Book, which informed him that the church had 1,029 members and that they paid 'the Church Keeper £400'.

How had Russell seen the Grafton Square church? He writes of it in his autobiography, *The Road Behind Me*, published in 1936, where he gives expression to various feelings, sometimes seemingly contradictory. In view of the busy life of the church and his involvement at every level, it is strange to read:

> In later years when a great London church made it difficult for me to do much, my wife spent most of her time in this way [i.e. getting into personal contact with the so-called 'depressed districts' instead of paying other people to let them forget about such places] amongst the people of the Mission we supported and manned in Wandsworth Road and her experience was similar to mine.[10]

The chapter which deals with his time in Clapham, entitled 'A Fellowship and a Friendship' gives eleven of its seventeen pages to his meeting Bishop Whelldon, Dean of Durham, and him inviting the dean to preach at Grafton Square. He then turns his attention to the church itself:

> My new church was a glorious building with great traditions... The church in his [Guinness Rogers'] time had enormous wealth, much of which was used to start unnecessary 'causes' in less affluent portions of the neighbourhood, and the only survival of these was the Mission in Wandsworth Road where my wife was to find her supreme joy amongst humble folk who are still her friends, and where the church still carries on, unaided and with great energy and sacrifice a magnificent and fruitful enterprise ... we had 'the downstairs people' who sat in pews of gorgeous oak with carved ends and received their pew-rent receipts by mail and the 'gallery people' who worshipped in unadorned pitch-pine and got their payments marked on a card in their seats.

This system originated in the days when gentry, families and guests sat downstairs and their servants were placed above.

Clearly, by 1915, the ban on wine imposed on the ladies by Mrs Guinness Rogers had been removed for, according to Russell:

> The Ladies Working Party met in the mornings over a glass of port, while the Dorcas Society assembled in the afternoons round a less aristocratic and inebriating cup of tea. We had two great gates, with a circular drive-way connecting them, to enable the carriages to deposit their illustrious worshippers, and the rather ample spaces make in these latter times a not unsatisfactory car-park for some half-dozen less pretentious vehicles.'[11]

Russell's comments on his three immediate predecessors make interesting reading; perhaps they reveal as much about the writer as they do about his subjects:

My immediate predecessor [W. Morton Barwell], a saintly little
man but without much 'punch' was, so a kind friend told me as
he laid linoleum in my new house, 'far too good for London'. A
little later he paid me the compliment of saying that I might 'fill
the bill very well'. Thus acquitted of superfluous and impeding
sanctity, I recalled that my predecessor had followed a light-
hearted heretic who had scattered Guinness Rogers' congregation
with some gusto, congratulated his Presbyterian neighbour on
the reinforcements he was sending him, and after wrecking the
church, deserted it and then the ministry... Each of these brethren
left behind him a contingent of tactless friends and a group of
enthusiastic enemies. In addition to these, many felt that after Dr
Guinness Rogers no one could hope to be more than a farthing
candle, feebly spluttering where that great luminary had spread
his rays, while others referred to him in very uncomplimentary
language, pronounced him abominably rude, resolute against
unfermented Communion wine – his brewery connections being
obvious in his name [Russell seems not to have been aware of the
attachment of Dr and Mrs Guinness Rogers to the temperance
cause] ... As a matter of fact Rogers was neither so great or so
small as his critics made him.

In his penultimate 'Minister's Letter' in the *Grafton News* of
July 1929, Russell tells the congregation that:

In entering the United Church of Canada, I follow my conviction
that mere sectarianism is out of date and is paralysing religion
in England. Church union is the burning question which must
be faced and which should begin with that wedding of the
Presbyterian and Congregational Churches, the first steps to which
I am proud to have led.

That marriage, incidentally, took place 42 years after the
writing of those words and fifteen years after the writer's
death, with the founding of the United Reformed Church in
England and Wales in 1972.

The pages of *Grafton News* for the summer months of 1929
devoted many pages to the saga of Stanley Russell's departure,
including not only the minister's letter, letters from deacons,

detailed reports of various farewell meetings and final services, but also a description of the Canadian church to which the Russells were heading, and of the welcome service there. *Grafton News* described Toronto as:

> ... the heart of its [Canada's] religious and intellectual life. The 'Queen City' has a very large population, almost entirely British, and Christian activities focus around the United Church of Canada... while Lake Ontario prevents the extension of the city in a southerly direction, growth northwards is possible and has produced a great residential district of beautiful homes, in the midst of which is Deer Park Church.

Formerly Presbyterian it is now a unit in the United Church in which Methodists, Presbyterians and Congregationalists have found a home.

As noted, in 1928 Deer Park Church had 1,029 members, a large number of young men and women in association, and many co-related activities.

> It has normally a Minister and an Assistant Minister and supports a missionary abroad. The buildings are modern and consequently much more 'ecclesiastical' in design that older Canadian churches. The robed choir of about fifty voices (including four soloists) leads the singing and the building will hold about 1,300 worshippers... In relinquishing Mr Russell, all connected with Grafton Square must find some consolation in the knowledge that he has been called to a service abounding in such magnificent opportunities for the exercise of his brilliant talents as a preacher and leader.

Two pages were allocated in a later issue of *Grafton News* to report in detail Russell's induction and first Sunday at his Canadian pastorate.

Russell spent the next 25 years at Deer Park where he played a prominent role in the life of the United Church of Canada. He gained a DD in 1934 from Victoria University, Toronto, and was awarded the same doctorate by Aberdeen University in 1938. In Canada he was chaplain to the Imperial

Service Veterans of Toronto from 1938. An ardent royalist, he wrote articles in Canada looking forward to the restoration of the European monarchies. He passed away just before his retirement date from Deer Park. An obituary note, probably from *The Christian World*, in the Clapham church's collection at the London Archives says that:

> He will be remembered by many in this country as a brilliant pulpit orator and an adventurous spirit in the field of theology… in Toronto he occupied a position of unchallenged supremacy among the preachers and Christian leaders of the city. Dr Russell had a richly stored mind and to 'sit under' him was to get a perpetually renewed vision of the colour and drama of Christian history and thought.

Such a man would be a hard act to follow in the best of circumstances!

Russell's biography reveals a complex character. It contains a strong element of name-dropping, not only in the chapter entitled 'Before they were famous'. Alongside this it is obvious that he has a great concern and compassion for the poor and underprivileged. Possibly, the most moving and personal chapter is that entitled 'Into the War and Out of It', in which he describes, as already noted, his work as a chaplain in a military hospital. He had started the Great War as a keen patriot, if not a jingoist, preaching a sermon with the text 'Curse ye Meroz' (from Judges 5.23). His chaplain experiences among young men who had suffered horribly at the Front put a firm end to that:

> Indeed, the whole thing viewed by any friend of youth, was so revolting and cruel, that it, more than anything else made me a pacifist… the idea that the lads were being killed for very different things from those so eloquently urged to defend [by politicians and preachers]; the obscenities of conscription (which is indistinguishable from slavery); the return to tribalism as the religion which camouflaged as Christianity encouraged our 'effort'…[12]

The chapter ends with these words: 'At any rate, if the beginning of the Great War found me delivering my soul on "Curse ye Meroz", the end of it found me securely established in the conviction regarding all war which Lincoln expressed about slavery, "If this is not wrong, nothing is wrong".'[13]

Stanley Russell died in 1957. The Revd Thomas Jarrett wrote of him in the *Christian World*:

> The passing of G. Stanley Russell removes one of the greatest of pulpit orators from the scene. It was as a schoolboy who dropped into Grafton-Square Church, Clapham, one Sunday evening over thirty years ago that I first saw Stanley Russell. That visit to Grafton Square left an indelible impression. The rich old oak pews, the music before the service which touched the soul to expectancy, the stately entrance of surpliced minister and choir, the reverence, order and beauty of the service opened my eyes to the wealth of devotion possible to a Congregational Church. If memory does not fail, Russell preached from 'Speak unto the children of Israel that they go forward'; and it was an utterance devout, profound, touching life at many points (and so incidentally revealing Russell's wide range of interests and broad understanding of history) and moving unimpeded by redundant words, phrases and ideas to the true and definite climax in Christ.' Another nameless British obituary said that he 'will be remembered by many in this country as a brilliant pulpit orator and an adventurous spirit in the field of theology... he occupied a position of unchallenged supremacy among the preachers and Christian leaders of the city [Toronto]. Dr Russell had a richly stored mind, and to 'sit under him' was to get a perpetually renewed vision of the colour and drama of Christian history and thought.

***

While Russell blossomed in Canada the Clapham church saw an immediate decline. According to John Drennan, his departure 'was a blow to the church at Grafton Square. Although the move was understandable, the effect was serious and congregations and financial contributions grew less.'

The departure of the much-loved and respected pastor left the Grafton Square church, and especially its diaconate, in a condition very similar to a deep sense of bereavement. People in such a condition are invariably advised not to rush into things – very wise counsel!

Unfortunately, the deacons seemed to be suffering from a state of panic, and were not wise. In just a couple of months John Drennan reported to his fellow deacons that:

> ... he had written to the Rev. J. Welham Clarke MA that the Pastorate Committee would recommend his name to the Church Meeting inviting him to the pastorate of the church. Mr Clarke had replied saying that he would carefully consider the call if a unanimous one. Dr Watts [deacon] would be seeing Mr Clarke in the course of a few days.

By mid-December 1929, less than five months after the departure of his predecessor, Welham Clarke had received the anticipated call, writing his letter of acceptance on 19 December. A deacons' letter to the congregation, dated 31 December, and probably written by the church secretary, informed the church that it was to have a new minister. It enabled its readers to see what had struck the deacons about the pastor they had called:

> He fully realises that we are offering him no sinecure. To follow so great a preacher as the Rev. G. Stanley Russell and so beloved a pastor and his wife requires a courage and determination which we appreciate and admire in both Mr and Mrs Clarke. Our minister-elect is a man of wide experience and sympathies. He set out on a business career, but after some years felt a call to the Ministry. He went accordingly to Lancashire College for training and preparation. The war intervened. He enlisted as a private in the R.A.M.C., saw service in Palestine and finished as a sergeant-major. His experience leaves him a lover of and fighter for peace. He is a strong supporter of the League of Nations and what it stands for... He has been Chairman for 1929 of the Warwickshire Congregational Union. He comes to us with good recommendations. Indeed, perhaps only those on the pastorate

committee realise that our decision to invite Mr Clarke was based
as much on these recommendations as on the excellent impression
he made when he conducted our services and preached on
November 17th. He impresses me as a man who loves and appeals
to children. I think our Sunday Schools will find him a great
support, and also that he will take a special interest in the work at
Grafton Hall. He has a great gift of organisation, and we have been
told from two independent sources that he is capable of a great
work. Let us all join with him in doing that great work at Grafton
Square.

Clearly neither deacons nor minister-elect had given much
consideration to such precipitated action!

John Welham Clarke MA BD was born in Lowestoft
on 23 August 1888, the son of George Ernest Clarke JP,
dental surgeon and church secretary of the London Road
Congregational Church, Lowestoft. His mother was the
daughter of the Revd H. Andrews of Woodbridge. After his
education at Lowestoft School, the Strand School, London,
and King's College, London, he worked for two years at
the Yarmouth branch of Lloyds Bank. He'd married Elsie
Richards at their home church of London Road.

He trained for the ministry at Lancashire Congregational
College and Manchester University, gaining his BA in 1912 and
MA in philosophy in 1913. His studies were interrupted by the
Great War, when he served with the YMCA (1914–15) and in
the Royal Army Medical Corps (1915–19). His ship bound for
Gallipoli was torpedoed and Clarke found himself in Egypt,
attached to the Egyptian Camel and Labour Corps. He was
mentioned in dispatches in this campaign.

At the end of the Great War he returned for a year to
Lancashire Congregational College, before being ordained in
1920. His pastorates were Salem Church, Burnley (1920–5);
Spencer Street, Leamington (1925–30); Clapham (1930–3) and
Fish Street Memorial Church, Hull (1933–43).

The Second World War brought severe bombing to Hull, with
the evacuation of many people causing churches to weaken

and the loss of ministers. Clarke undertook the supervision of the remaining churches there, having as many as five in his care. Later he served Winston Magna, Braunton, Devon (1949–52); and Newark (1952 until his retirement in 1955). He was chairman of the Warwickshire Congregational Union (1925–6). He published *Three Religious Plays*.

John Drennan wrote this about his time in Clapham:

> Although he was a good minister in many ways, he faced an impossible task in following Dr Russell. The situation in Clapham was not propitious and many of Dr Russell's followers drifted away quickly. The situation grew worse when the Deacons recommended Mr Clarke to seek another pastorate. He was to receive part salary with the use of the Manse until he was settled.

When she read these words in a copy of *Grafton News* in the late 1960s, Mr Clarke's widow was most upset, stating that he had not been dismissed, but had resigned. The minutes of deacons' and church meetings, together with various items of correspondence, provide a detailed account.[14]

One incident which would have probably upset a powerful element in the church occurred in April 1930 and received worldwide coverage, including in *The Straits Times* of Singapore. An article in the 25 April issue was headed: 'CHURCH BAN ON JEW. Forbidden to take part of Christ.' This reported Welham Clarke's refusal to allow Maurice Bannister, librarian of the Zionist Organisation in London, to take the part of Christ in a Lenten cantata. Bannister had been invited to do so some weeks earlier by church organist Richard Jevons, and rehearsals were under way. The deacons' meeting had decided unanimously not to permit Bannister to sing this part. Welham Clarke commented:

> We felt it would be quite incongruous for a Jew to take such a part... There is no political, personal or racial feeling in this. It is merely a question of religion... This is a religious service and not a concert. It would take place in the church, and we felt that it

would hurt the feelings of many of the congregation if they knew that a Jew was singing the words which were supposed to have been uttered by Christ. In any case it would be impossible for Mr Bannister to be sincere in rendering such a part. Being a Jew by religion, he does not believe in Jesus Christ in the same way we do. The words that he would be singing would express thoughts which are quite contrary to his own faith... We would not object to his taking the part of any other character in the cantata and, as a matter of fact, one of the artists engaged for a forthcoming rendering of Bach's *Matthew Passion* is a Jew. We have no prejudice against Jews as such.[15]

Nonetheless, despite the unanimous vote of the deacons, it was the minister who made the statement to the press; it was his name which would be associated with the ban and, doubtless, the criticism of the organist and many associated with performing the cantata would fall on his head.

According to church minutes the deacons met in January 1933 to share their concern about 'signs of depression and lack of leadership' in the church. There was no suggestion that, perhaps, their minister needed their pastoral care. Two representatives of the deacons then met with the minister and advised him in confidence that:

> ... in view of his apparent depression and unhappiness and lack of confidence so essential to church leadership, he should undertake more preaching engagements outside and so possibly find a sphere of work more suited to him; he insisted on seeing the actual resolution agreed at the deacons' meeting in his absence.

Unrest and dissatisfaction grew as the year went on, with a falling-off in attendances and a serious decline in finances. The deacons noted that some of the most regular attendees had stopped coming; it is likely that these were the people who had lamented most the departure of their beloved Stanley Russell. The deacons were deeply troubled too that church income in 1932 was £200 less than in 1929 (the year of Russell's departure). Membership had seen a drop of 47 in three years too.

However, the criticism was not all directed at the minister. The deacons were concerned at an undercurrent of negative criticism aimed at them, arising from rumours concerning the January meeting noted above which stated that a harmful atmosphere had been created in the church. The task of the deacons, they felt, had been made more difficult, and they were weary of the burden and anxiety laid upon them, insisting that they themselves were the most loyal attendees at church services and meetings and that they had truly endeavoured to give the minister support at all times. Matters came to a head at the deacons' meeting on 18 September 1933 when a letter of resignation from a married couple was received. It was agreed that two deacons should visit them in an attempt to get them to reconsider. There was a letter too from a Mr Digby, 'stating that in view of adverse criticism from some members of the congregation regarding the conduct of Church affairs by the Deacons, he felt it would be in the best interests of the Minister and the Church if a vote of confidence in the Deacons be asked for at the next Church Meeting.' The Revd Welham Clarke then said that if this letter were brought to the church meeting:

> ... it would make his position more intolerable than ever and he
> considered that the best way out of the difficulty would be for him
> to resign the pastorate... It was agreed that a committee [probably
> of some deacons and church members] undertake the matter
> and report to the Deacons their recommendation. Mr Clarke's
> proposal would mean that a special circular would be sent to every
> member of the Congregation calling for a special Church Meeting
> for Thursday October 5th 1933 to consider his proposal and also
> that the 2 Sundays' legal notice be given out in the Church, Sept.
> 25 and Oct. 1st This was agreed and Mr Clarke left the meeting.
> Mr Adams took the chair and the matter was fully discussed, and
> it was unanimously agreed that Mr Clarke's suggestion that he
> should resign the pastorate should be recommended to the Church
> for confirmation, and that there was no other course open but
> to accept his suggestion. It was agreed that the Secretary should
> telephone Mr Clarke in the morning asking him to send the letter
> which he proposed [this method was Mr Clarke's own suggestion].

Welham Clarke wrote his letter next day and this was discussed by the deacons in his absence on 23 September. Their reply informed him of the calling of a special church meeting to discuss the matter. They then decided unanimously to recommend that the church accept the resignation. Correspondence between senior deacons Percy Adams and Fred Lovett shows the sense of ill-ease and uncertainty which trouble the diaconate.

The special church meeting on 5 October listened to the minister reading his letter of resignation, in which he declared:

> It is a letter which I feel I must write; and it would ill behove me who have so often urged others to do their duty without fear and in faith of God's goodness to fail myself when duty calls. I have for a long time been conscious of grave unrest and dissatisfaction in certain quarters of the church, and in spite of my efforts and prayers that unrest and dissatisfaction have increased so as to render real aggressive Christian work on my part at any rate quite impossible. Also I have been greatly disturbed by the fact that the finances of the church are (I understand) in a very precarious condition, and that a crisis is fast approaching. Such knowledge has not only occasioned great unhappiness to me but I discover it is now getting on my nerves to such an extent that I feel in danger of a nervous collapse in the near future unless the strain, now well-nigh intolerable, is relieved. And there is only one way in which relief and peace can be found. I shall be glad therefore if you will place my resignation from the pastorate of the church before the members at the Special Meeting which this letter will necessitate – such resignation to take place immediately. This course has not been taken in any light mood (you know, in fact, that I have contemplated such action before) and the family responsibilities devolving upon me as a married man with three young children make this a very serious step (fraught with grave risks not nobly to myself but to others very dear to me). Yet I feel it is a step which must be bravely taken, and I shall go forth with faith in God that all will be for the best. I trust that you will urge the acceptance of this resignation, not only for my own sake, but still more for the sake of the peace, unity and prosperity of the church; and I

pray that under new leadership in the days to come, the Church at Grafton Square may go forward unitedly and happily, to do the work and will of God.

When the deacons presented their motion that the resignation be accepted, it was met with a mixed reaction. Several people expressed surprise at the situation; others, sympathetic to the minister, felt nevertheless that he could not operate without the full confidence of the whole church. One expressed her unhappiness that Mr Clarke had been forced to resign, and would not support the motion. Others were concerned that the church meeting was being kept in the dark or that the talk of dissatisfaction should have been discussed at a church meeting – one had heard from a friend in the Midlands that the minister had been asked to leave. Eventually the meeting was persuaded to accept the minister's resignation because he wished it. Minister and church had been damaged by what had happened.

One cannot help note the similarity of the situations in which Stanley Russell's predecessor and successor found themselves in Grafton Square. Both appear to have been pressurised by their deacons to leave. Welham Clarke died on 29 November 1965. His obituary in the *Congregational Year Book* for 1966 states:

> He was a brilliant preacher with a voice of outstanding quality to the end. He was a great pioneer and spared no effort to reach the people wherever he lived. Old and young alike loved him and he was especially popular talking with children... He is remembered with loyalty and affection in all the churches he served.

There were some people remaining in Clapham in the 1960s who thought highly of him. One of his 'sins', in the deacons' eyes, was that he tried to bring together the church in Old Town, Clapham, and the mission on the Wandsworth Road – an idea quite unacceptable to the class-bound deacons.

According to John Drennan, 'the break with Mr Clarke

greatly upset the church and many members protested. Numbers had now fallen from several hundred to one hundred and less.' This was due, of course, not only to the church's troubled story but also to the tendency of people in the area to move out further from London.

In his 1915 church manual letter, Stanley Russell had written, 'I must be myself, not any of my predecessors or contemporaries, and I am quite sure that in Clapham you will give me the right atmosphere of encouragement, co-operation and prayer – in which any ability that I may have may be enabled to find the channels through which it can best serve God and you.'

A main factor in the tragic situation of 1933 was that the deacons and members of Grafton Square only looked for another Stanley Russell.

15

Lean Days

Two years passed before the arrival of the Revd Arthur Halfpenny MA in 1935. The son of Congregational minister John Arthur Halfpenny, then serving at Watton, Norfolk, he was born on 28 August 1906. Educated at Caterham and Oxford University, he graduated in History, before his ministerial training at Mansfield College. He was ordained at Headgate Congregational Church, Colchester, in 1930. John Drennan reports that:

> Mr Halfpenny was a good preacher and a most sincere Christian. He was a pacifist. He attracted young people and many aspects of his ministry were very happy... Church attendance was not very good. The choir had gone and, with twenty or thirty people, the big church looked empty. The size of congregations reflects both the catastrophic decline in membership during the 1930s and the social changes taking place in Clapham as wealthy inhabitants moved further out from London and their large houses gradually were taken over for multi-occupation.

Mr Halfpenny suggested holding the services in the church hall, which was more suitable, and the congregation agreed.

To assist the church, he became a locum teacher of history at Harrow Weald County School on 5 October 1939, and a month later this became a full-time appointment for the duration of the war. He remained on the school's staff until 1967 and his wife Edith also taught there. It became necessary for them to live nearer the school and so they moved to Harrow. It was

Revd Leslie Artingstall

announced that he would be available to lead worship on only two Sundays a month thereafter. The outbreak of war in 1939 had added to the church's difficulties as people were evacuated, but services continued in the hall. During the war Mr Halfpenny thought that he should resign for various reasons but was 'persuaded to continue to taking pulpit services'. He eventually left the Clapham church in 1951. It is said in his obituary in the *Congregational Year Book* in 1992 that 'His preaching was always direct and challenging and not without humour. An uncompromising pacifist, he often discussed the working out of the Gospel in modern society.' His first wife, to whom he was married for 50 years, predeceased him. Arthur Halfpenny died on 14 April 1991 and was survived by his second wife, Phyllis.

It was arranged that Sunday services at Clapham would be shared in 1941. The Revd Leslie Artingstall was born in Manchester on 14 February 1885. He gained his BA degree from Victoria University, Manchester, and trained for the ministry at Lancashire Congregational College. After holding pastorates at Trinity, Swinton (1911–16) and Fleetwood (1916–19), he joined the staff of the LMS, serving as district secretary for the northern counties (1919–28) and as organising secretary (1936–7). In 1937, with the shadow of war over Europe, Artingstall became secretary of the Fellowship of Reconciliation, from which he resigned in 1946, a year after the end of the Second World War.

Artingstall became co-pastor with Arthur Halfpenny on 19 January 1941, conducting two services a month and undertaking some pastoral work. It was decided to hold evening services only in summer months. In 1945 he began a three-year pastorate at Pevensey Road Congregational Church, Eastbourne, leaving that post to serve as a field officer of the Sussex Congregational Union (1948–50). Leslie Artingstall died in Eastbourne on 19 October 1952. His obituary in the 1953 *Congregational Year Book* describes him as:

> ... a true and faithful minister of the Gospel, passionate for the truth, a brilliant organizer, an indefatigable worker, and a man with a deep concern for people in all parts of the world... He conceived of the mission of the Church in large terms, his vision was always spacious. And yet while moving in large spheres of thought and objective he never neglected needs and responsibilities close at hand... He had the gift of friendliness to a marked degree. Nothing could keep him from the service of the Church and it is typical that he should have been on the way to a meeting at the time of the onslaught of his fatal illness.

The fact that this church was served by two pacifist ministers during the ten years following 1935 is surely worthy of note. Stanley Russell had become a pacifist during the Great War as a result of ministering to young wounded soldiers. Support for the pacifist position grew during the Great War and the jingoism of 1914 weakened as the casualty lists grew and people became aware of the horrors of the situation in France.

This change is also reflected in the writings of English and Welsh poets during the conflict. Anti-war feeling grew during the 1920s and early 1930s and is exemplified by 'The King and Country' debate at the Oxford Union on 9 February 1933. The motion: 'That this House will in no circumstances fight for its King and Country' was passed by 275 votes to 153. The mood in the country began to change by about 1935, influenced by the rise of Fascism in Spain and Italy, and Nazism in Germany.

***

The church building did not remain unscathed through the war. On 5 October 1940 a police office interrupted a deacons' meeting to report that the steeple was in a dangerous state as the result of an air raid. On 2 November another bomb caused damage to church windows, the ceiling of the deacons' vestry and to the church hall, while Belmont Hall also suffered damage. Ultimate destruction came on a Saturday night in January 1945, on the eve of the church anniversary services. Church members claim that this was the last V2 rocket to fall on London. Arthur Halfpenny recalled the scene they saw next morning, in *Grafton News*, March 1968:

> I well remember that Sunday morning when we arrived at church only to find that the building itself had been turned into a shattered shell, irretrievably damaged by a blast from a bomb which had dropped nearby during the night. We stood outside feeling pretty gloomy, and some of the most devoted members of the church, who had served it faithfully for years, had tears in their eyes. Then Mr Webber, the organist, in spite of our warnings of the danger of falling debris, determined to find out if the organ[1] was still working, put on his 'tin-hat', went into the building and, in a few moments, the strains of 'Onward Christian Soldiers' came floating out fortissimo into the Square, much to the astonishment of passers-by.

Mrs E. M. Ware, a church member since 1907, and a lady of indomitable spirit, remembered it thus in the same magazine:

> On a Sunday morning in 1945, the blow fell and our beloved church was destroyed. We could no longer use it for worship, a sad time for the Revs. Arthur Halfpenny and Leslie Artingstall, the co-pastors. Mr Webber, our organist, found to his delight that the organ was not damaged, and played 'Onward Christian Soldiers' for all to hear. Then to work, to clear and clean, and make ready for future services: this, a small party of older members, men and women, set to work with determination. The Congregational

143

'cathedral' was damaged beyond repair. Its ruin had to be demolished and the small congregation had to face the task of creating a temporary home in a small rear hall and the greater task of rebuilding. It did so without hesitation and with manifest courage.

It seems worth adding a comment made by Mrs Ware in the 1970s: 'Weren't we lucky! It was the last V2 of the war. It could have missed us. Poor Balham, left with that great barn of a place to care for while we have a lovely and more suitable modern building.'

The arrangement of two co-ministers only covered Sunday services with, as noted, some pastoral work of a limited nature being undertaken by Artingstall. Pastoral care therefore became the responsibility of the ladies of the church, led by Mrs Ware. But despite all these endeavours it became clear that the church needed a full-time minister and the arrangement with Messrs Halfpenny and Artingstall came to an end.

John Drennan sums up the situation: 'The prospect was not a tempting one for any man, with a ruined church building and a membership reduced to about sixty. However the spirit was good and the financial prospect was encouraging.'

16

Rising
from the Ashes

AT LENGTH, IN 1952, with considerable courage, the Revd James Elvan Harris agreed to come to lead the church in a difficult new era, one which would include the challenge of building of a new church.

Harris was born 13 March 1909, the son of the Revd Gomer Harris, Congregational minister of Llangynidr, Breconshire. After schooling in Caterham, he spent a brief period doing office work before training for the ministry at the Congregational Memorial College, Brecon. Ordained in Machen in 1939, he was pastor of the church there until 1941, when he moved to Penmaenmawr.

He became a Royal Navy chaplain in 1943, seeing service in the Far East and being one of the first people to enter Japanese prisoner-of-war camps in Singapore. After being discharged from the Navy in 1946, he became minister of Paddock Congregational Church, Huddersfield, leaving there in 1952 for Clapham, where he was minister throughout the whole period of planning and constructing a new church building. He was a keen Rotarian, being president of the Clapham association. In 1965 he moved to West Kensington, from where he retired, briefly to Leeds, before settling in Thame, Oxfordshire, where he died on 21 November 1977. In 1942 he had married Catherine Evelyn Lewis who by the time of their stay in Clapham held a senior post in the National Health Service in London.

Revd James Elvan Harris

The post-war period was one of planning and reconstruction in Clapham as in the rest of the war-ravaged world. Meetings took place with the Congregational moderator for London and officials at Memorial Hall, the headquarters of the Congregational Union of England and Wales. An architect was appointed and various designs were prepared and discussed. There were also meetings with officials from the War Damage Commission and many church discussions on fundraising. John Drennan provides the details:

After much haggling the [War Damage] Fund agreed to provide £26,000. This was about half the value of the church destroyed but was based on the requirements of the existing congregation, which was a maximum of 250. Fortunately the Fund did agree that the stained glass windows destroyed were of value and agreed to provide £1,600 in replacement.

It was said in the 1960s that an attempt was made to obtain this sum in cash but that the Fund refused, saying that it had to be 'windows for windows'. In the event, the window provided was beautiful indeed. Drennan continues:

Belmont Hall had also been damaged and was sold to London County Council for £3,000. The Council also wished to buy the Mission Hall in the Wandsworth Road as part of a housing project and generously gave £10,000 for the site, so as to include the provision of a new hall in the new church complex. The congregation by various means raised £800, whilst the Organ Fund had £1,000 for the sale of the organ. The London Congregational Union gave the somewhat disappointing sum of £1,000. However, the total available for all purposes came to about £42,500.

Deer Park Church, Toronto, presented £150 to provide a pulpit as a tribute to Dr Stanley Russell, minister at Clapham before moving to Deer Park, while Dr and Mrs Russell presented the great Cross in the chancel. The organ in the old building had been sold, and reconditioned and installed in the restored parish church of All Saints, Poplar in the 1950s.

Building work began in 1956 and, in the meantime, the church struggled to carry on its activities in limited conditions: Sunday worship, a small Sunday school, Boys' Brigade and Women's Own (which had transferred from the Wandsworth Road Mission Hall when that was closed). The fine new complex, with a church to hold 250, a large hall with a stage, classrooms, vestries, excellent kitchen, and five sets of toilets (men, women, boys, girls and minister) was opened at a service conducted by the Revd Howard Stanley, secretary of the Congregational Union of England and Wales, on 8 March 1958.

During the ministry of Elvan Harris the church struggled to find its feet once more. The choir was re-established; Guides and Brownies were set up alongside the Boys' Brigade, and various social events were arranged to deepen fellowship and build up relationships.

The minister's departure to West Kensington in 1965 brought yet another vacancy but this was quickly filled by the coming of an interim minister in the person of the Revd George Harold Shaw, a retired Congregationalist minister. Shaw was born in Sheffield in 1892 and trained for the ministry at Paton College, Nottingham. He served pastorates at Halstead (1928–32); Hammersmith Broadway (1932–43); Newark (1943–8) and Heston from 1948 until his retirement in 1963. He and his wife, though still living at Heston, showed great care to

The new
church,
1958
John Roper

The pulpit – a gift from Deer Park Church, Toronto

the Clapham congregation in its time of need and gave it the support it needed during the vacancy. The next minister was told more than once that, had George Shaw been available, he would not have been considered.

Then, in 1967, another Welshman, the Revd Ivor Thomas Rees BA DipTh, minister of a Welsh Independent church in Port Talbot, was inducted to the pastorate. Son of a Rhondda coal miner and a graduate of the University of Wales he, like his predecessor, trained in Brecon. On his first visit to Clapham he was taken to lunch and then driven around the district by church secretary John Roper who drew his attention to all of its less attractive features. At an informal meeting that evening, Roper and the other deacons spoke at length about the church's problems and were anxious to answer any questions. When asked whether they had questions, John Roper replied, 'Oh, no! We believe that if we share our problems with a minister and then he comes, we regard that as the call of God.'

In the event, of course, though the church had its back against the wall, things were not as bleak as they had described. When Rees arrived the membership was 67, rising to 73 in six years. The really active people included a number of adherents who gladly agreed to church membership on being approached. Average adult attendance at morning worship varied between 30 and 45, with about 30 children, many of whom were of Afro-Caribbean parentage. The three youth organisations – Guides, Boys' Brigade and Youth Club – were active.

The Women's Own, led by Mrs Ware, met each week and had transferred to Grafton Square from the Wandsworth Road. Known locally as 'Mrs Ware's Meeting', there remained a little of the ethos from Victorian and Edwardian days described so graphically by Miss Hilda Drennan. Though she held no office in the church at that time, Mrs Ware was, nonetheless, an important figure, and one of the few older people who remembered the 'great days of Grafton'. It was she who had sole charge of the church's silverware. By then the word 'silverware' had become somewhat debased by the American talk of plastic silverware, but this was the real thing. The set contained every kind of knife, fork and spoon, each of solid silver and wrapped lovingly in its own chamois leather. It appeared only on the most special occasions, and only Mrs Ware was allowed to handle it in the unwrapping, washing and re-wrapping stages.

There was also a monthly social gathering called Square Circle, which was meant to suggest that anyone could fit in. To these meetings the new minister added a weekly Bible study.

The church in 1967 was a very different place from that described in earlier pages. Indeed Clapham itself had changed. The small congregation consisted of two main groups for the most part: elderly people whose membership went back 60 years or more and who remembered the large congregations and bustling activity of yesteryear, and those who were newcomers to church life. There was also a sprinkling of people who had come from churches elsewhere. The church struggled, but there was a determination to overcome difficulties and work together to build for the future, allied with a willingness to experiment. The new minister found it hard to realise that when he was told, 'You're the governor', it was meant.

One name stands out above all others in the post-war period, that of church secretary A. J. Roper. In many ways John Roper represented the best in the church's tradition. For many years he was head of the British office of Maersk Shipping Company and was also the London representative of several Norwegian shipping companies. John and his wife Rene were raised at the Lavender Hill Church in Stormont Road but left there in 1950. He spoke little about it but it seemed that there had been a major disagreement and a number of people had left. The Ropers threw themselves into the life of the church in Grafton Square, where John soon became a deacon and then church secretary.

John Roper was a man of great integrity in every aspect of his life and possessed a quiet humour. He gave wise counsel and strong leadership without seeking to impose his views. A great friend and staunch supporter of his ministers, he always backed their initiatives, though always ready to offer wise counsel and, in at least one case, educate the minister in 'London ways'. A shy and humble person, he hid his many acts of generosity to ministers and less well-off families in the congregation. Even after he and Rene moved to Esher, he continued to attend morning and evening worship each Sunday for many years and to support all the church's main weekday events. He, more than any other person, guided the church through the long and difficult process of planning and then constructing its new buildings. The church was fortunate too that the few remaining rooms in the old building had been converted into a flat which was occupied by the caretakers Mr and Mrs Johnson who gave faithful service for several decades.

The Clapham of the late 1960s and early 1970s was in many ways an exciting place, with a wide spectrum of national, racial and class backgrounds. Wealth and poverty lived side by side. One cul-de-sac containing the residences of ambassadors and members of the aristocracy was overlooked by a block of council flats. The large residences in Grafton Square and on North Side of the Common were by now multi-occupied.

The first sign of even further change in the area appeared in the Peabody Estate across the Wandsworth Road in Battersea, where terraced houses for working-class people were bought up by new residents who could not afford to buy on the north side of the Thames. The Rolls Royce and Mercedes cars parked outside seemed as long as the house-fronts themselves in what became known as 'South Chelsea'. Back in the early 1970s a policeman on the Clapham beat spoke of some examples of Rachmanism[1] in the locality. Some residents were offered sums of money to move out. When they refused, they were visited late at night by men with large dogs.

The large residences on North Side too were being restored to their former glory. The whole of Grafton Square was sold in an auction at the Dorchester Hotel and that was shown later on a television programme in the early Seventies. The first house to be sold cost £12,000. The church caretaker, Johnny Johnson, was appalled, exclaiming, 'At the beginning of the war these were slums!' In 2012 the asking price for a two-bedroom flat in a Grafton Square house was £750,000. One wondered what had happened to all those families who were moved out.

Meanwhile, this was a period of increased ecumenical activity in the whole of Clapham. Initially this was organised by the Ministers' Fraternal, which was composed of some six Anglicans and the Congregational minister, who was made to feel at home very quickly. A special relationship developed between the Congregationalist church and minister and the clergy and congregation of Holy Trinity Parish Church, which had become home to the Clapham Sect. The large Roman Catholic Church of St Mary, served by Redemptorist Fathers, became involved too. Four priests, two young and two older, came to the Ministers' Fraternal where, for some time, the other members sat back to listen to heated debates between the two pairs of priests about the future of the Church. The Old Town churches (Anglican, Methodist, Roman Catholic and Congregational/URC) worshipped together regularly and shared Wednesday evening meetings in Lent. There was also the 15-mile sponsored walk in aid of Christian Aid around the borough boundaries of Lambeth and Wandsworth. Several Clapham clergy took part, including the URC minister.

Other changes were afoot at the same time. In 1968 the Seebohm Report on the social services was published. This recommended the abolition of separate social service departments – children's welfare, welfare of the elderly and physically handicapped and mental welfare, plus the home-help service – to be replaced by one social service department headed by a director. The department would be organised on a geographical basis rather than by the old categories. Each town or community would have an area office led by a manager and deputy. All social workers, whatever their background, would become 'generic' social workers, regarded as being qualified to handle any case allocated to them. The Conservative government accepted the Seebohm Report, announcing that the new pattern would come into effect in 1970. The Council of the Metropolitan Borough of Lambeth could not wait, and established a prototype area office in Clapham in 1968/9. At the same time, Clapham was chosen by the Metropolitan Police for an experimental scheme in which bobbies were put back on the beat. The local library too was chosen for a pioneer scheme in community service, of a wider scope than merely lending books.

In 1968/9, at the instigation of the area head of social services, every group involved in social care in the community (apart from the local doctors) came together to seek ways of working together. The Clapham Social Workers/Clergy Group was established, the first of its kind in Britain. Meetings for the first two years were held at the Grafton Square church before they transferred to the new area office. The founder-secretary was the Congregational minister. At some of the early meetings several of the younger social workers expressed guilt at living outside their area of work in what they described as 'more comfortable locations', at which the rector of Clapham gently commented that 'we are always here'. A memorable meeting was addressed by one of the country's first geriatricians, based in Greenwich. The address by the newly-elected Conservative MP for Clapham – the constituency sadly disappeared in 1974 – was equally memorable. Out of this activity grew such projects as the Youth Accommodation Project (Operation Short Stay), the Adventure Playground Project and a Door-to-Door Social Survey.

Alongside this joint activity was an agenda drawn up by the churches. Annual conferences were held to discuss renewal and similar topics, with never less than 80 people attending. The 1969 conference led to the setting up of a Helping Hands' scheme. The 1970 conference, entitled, 'Clapham – The Caring Community' proved to be an outstanding occasion. Over 100 people from local churches attended, together with representatives from Lambeth Social Services and other agencies. Among these was the director of social services for

Lambeth, who asked 'Who are all these people?' When he was told that they were Christians from local churches who were concerned for their community, he commented, 'I would not be able to persuade social workers to give up a Saturday for something like this.'

With the retirement of Methodist minister Leslie Webb, father of Methodist lay preacher Pauline,[2] a year or so after Ivor Rees arrived, the Methodists redrew circuit boundaries because of ministerial shortages, transferring their Clapham churches from the Lambeth area to the Wandsworth area. Ministers were unhappy about this development; indeed, the first to be appointed left the ministry as a result. Clapham played a secondary part in their ministries now and this resulted in the Grafton Square minister playing an increasingly solo ministerial role in the growing co-operation between the two churches. They now shared worship on Christmas Eve and Christmas Day, Holy Week and Good Friday, and evening services during January and August. This pattern continued for about four years and it appeared as though a union of the two causes was on the cards but, sadly, the Methodists were totally unwilling to open any discussions which might have led to the union of the two congregations. One Methodist comment was, 'We would never dream of leaving the High Street.' The irony of the situation was that the Grafton Square minister was quite confident that his church could have moved to the High Street site if only the Methodists had been more open to discussion. Ivor Rees' successor, the Revd Olive Symes, recalls, 'There was some talk of joining with the Methodists in the High Street but, when the chips were down, they really didn't want to know.' One can only dream of what might have been had this church union come about in the heart of Clapham. Sadly, none of Olive Symes' successors make any reference to the Methodist Church in the notes they provided to the author.

For two months in the summer of 1971 Clapham Congregationalists and their minister shared in a transatlantic pastoral exchange with the East Congregational Church of

Revd Ivor Thomas Rees   Revd Olive Symes
Ian Symes

Milton, Massachusetts, a congregation in the United Church of Christ. Its pastor, the Revd Malcolm E. Washburn Jr, was a guest of honour at a civic lunch arranged by the mayor of Lambeth, and it was seen as a sign of the good relationship between the Clapham churches and the civic authority. Ivor Rees later served as Chaplain for the Day to the Massachusetts House of Representatives, and the Rees family was delighted to meet the father of Mrs Washburn, a thirteen-generation direct descendent of John Robinson who preached to the Pilgrim Fathers. Churches, ministers and their families all agreed that this was indeed a worthwhile project.

17

Joining Together

As HAS BEEN noted, during the period when Stanley Russell was minister of Clapham Congregational Church he was involved in discussions suggesting a union of the Presbyterian Church of England and the then Congregational Union of England and Wales. The latter had been established in 1862 at the bicentenary of the Great Ejection to give impetus to evangelism and church extension.

Some voices called for a union with another denomination. Consideration was given to joining the Baptist Union of Great Britain and Ireland, and a joint Congregational/Baptist Assembly was actually held in 1901 but the matter seems to have ended there. The late 1920s discussions mentioned above failed too. The question was reopened after the Second World War and it was also revived in the 1960s, but it became apparent that discussions of a union with a national church presented difficulties. The result was that in 1965 Congregationalists voted to turn the Congregational Union of England and Wales into the Congregational Church in England and Wales, and the new body came into being in the following year.

Discussions at denominational and area levels (province/ presbytery), as well as in local churches, led to the publication of a Scheme of Union. For Presbyterians the vote of the General Assembly was sufficient and no local church in mainland Britain took advantage of the right to secede. But, the agreement of Congregational church meetings was needed, and the vast majority agreed, though sadly some 300 felt unable to go forward. The Clapham church meeting on 22 September 1971 voted unanimously in favour of supporting the formation of the United Reformed Church.

A service to close the activity of the Streatham district of the London Congregational Union was held at Balham, with the Clapham minister presiding as the last district chairman, and the Revd Dr John Huxtable as preacher. Huxtable was general secretary of the Congregational Church in England and Wales, later becoming the first joint secretary of the United Reformed Church.

The local service to mark the founding of the United Reformed Church took place at the former Presbyterian church of St Andrew's, Battersea Rise, and was attended by people from both the Congregational district and all the other Clapham churches. The Clapham minister presided and the guest preacher was the representative of the United Church of Christ in the USA at the founding assembly and Westminster Abbey service, the Revd Dr Allen Hackett, area minister for metropolitan Boston, Massachusetts, whom Ivor Rees had met in 1971.

Two years later Ivor Rees informed the church that he'd accepted a call to Ewell, Surrey, and the church once more faced a vacancy.

18

Grand Finale

WITHIN A YEAR of Ivor Rees' departure, the church received its first female minister in the person of the Revd Olive Doreen Symes from nearby New Malden. She had been trained under the Congregational Roll of Ministers' examination scheme, and was ordained in Clapham where she served from 1974 to 1982, adding Earlsfield Road to the pastorate (1976–82). Her second and last pastorate was at Haywards Heath (1982–80). She died 11 January 2012, aged 88.

It is interesting to recall that during this period, no less than five female ministers were neighbours in the inner London part of the Wimbledon district, while all the outer suburban and Surrey town churches were served by men.

In an undated letter received by the author in late 2011, Olive Symes shows her obvious surprise and pleasure at the ethnic mix of the congregation at Clapham; two of the elders were of West Indian origin. She speaks for her colleagues in praising the loyalty and work of the resident caretakers, Vi and Johnny Johnson, who had served the church well during at least three ministries. She also extols the virtues of church secretary John Roper, of 'a very supportive congregation', and the choir, 'such a small number of very good voices – they really did the church proud with their anthems'.

Olive Symes was followed by another woman coming to her first pastorate. Ann Maureen Cole had trained at Westminster College, Cambridge, and was ordained in Clapham in 1983 and inducted to the pastorate of Clapham and the church at

Battersea Road. In a 2011 letter she described the Clapham congregation as consisting of:

> ... the old, indigenous white Londoners and a large West Indian community. They brought a joy to worship and relationships were excellent between the two groups... That did not go down well with certain political activists. One night the beautiful church was desecrated – covered in swastikas inside and out – graffiti – torn-up Bibles, smashed font, obscenities everywhere. But within an hour of the police coming for me, the printers next door came in with their special chemicals and cleaned the lot. Father Charlie from the Roman Catholic Church [St Mary's] came to offer us the use of their hall for our services. The District and Synod supported in other ways and we were re-dedicated in a couple of weeks. Church life carried on. During my last year we had a request from Korean exiled Christians living in London to use our church. This became a regular Sunday afternoon service and I attended often. Hymns would be printed in English and Korean and much joy was shared in the name of the Lord.[1]

During 1986–7 the Revd Ann Cole was asked to serve two more churches, those at Earlsfield and Battersea Bridge Road, creating a four-church pastorate. 'I knew that I couldn't do that,' and in 1987 she accepted a call to Seaford, where she served until her retirement in 1998, adding the Alfriston church to her ministerial responsibility in 1993. Ann Cole commented: 'My training ground! – I loved it. Clapham accepted me, cared and loved us both.'

Brian Leonard Eyles trained at Western College, Bristol, graduating BA and MPhil from that city's university. Ordained in 1967, he ministered at Blacon (1967–77) and Staplehurst and Maidstone (1977–87) before moving to London in the year of Ann Cole's departure to be involved in creating the Commons Group consisting of four churches: Clapham; St Andrew's, Battersea; Earlsfield; and East Hill, Wandsworth. Eyles ministered in the pastorate until he moved to another group of churches in east Coventry in 2002. He retired in 2005.

A colleague for Eyles arrived one year later in 1988. Egland Graham had trained for the ministry at the Jamaica Bible Seminary before crossing the Atlantic to Northern College, Manchester. Ordained in 1980, he served pastorates in Saffron Lane, Leicester, and Tottenham before moving to Clapham. Here he became joint pastor with Brian Eyles in the Commons Group. He discovered a church in Clapham which was thoroughly integrated, with two church secretaries (one black and one white) as well as two ministers (one black and one white). He welcomed the local ecumenical activity and particularly appreciated the excellent relationship with the parish church and its rector. Graham moved to Christ Church, Enfield (1999–2001) and thence to Acton Hill in 2001, from where he retired in 2004.

When Graham left Clapham another team member arrived in the person of non-stipendiary minister, the Revd Mary Read, a member at Ewell URC, whose current minister was Ivor Rees, formerly of Clapham. Like her husband, Professor Jim Reed, the first professor of comparative law at the School of Oriental and African Studies, University of London, she was a native of Gwent. Both developed a great love for Africa during the time when Jim taught law in Tanzania, but they were unable to fulfil their dream of returning to their beloved continent. Ordained within the Wimbledon district in 1991, she served as an auxiliary minister in the Commons Group (1991–7).

Another ordination took place in the pastorate in 1995, with the arrival from Northern College, Manchester, of Alexander [Alex] David Mabbs, a graduate of Manchester University. The ministerial team was reorganised, with Eyles concentrating on St Andrew's and East Hill, Mabbs in Clapham and Earlsfield, while Mary Read ministered across the whole group. By now the membership at Clapham church had dropped to 20, with slightly fewer at Sunday services, but the robed choir, now a quartet, continued to make its full contribution to worship. The Junior Church was still of a reasonable size. All-age services were held once a month and there was excitement at receiving into membership six young people, three of whom were baptised by immersion in a portable baptistry. The church continued to pull its weight ecumenically in what was in the late 1990s 'a strong and active group, whose activities included supporting a residential project for refugee women, a Roman Catholic outreach to the homeless and resourcing a community project on Clapham's Notre Dame estate, employing a community development worker and a youth worker.'[2]

During this period a number of members, including several officers, died. The Clapham church looked seriously at its future with several factors influencing its thinking. St Andrew's URC, just a mile away, had undergone major refurbishment over a period of two years, when its congregation worshipped at East Hill church, Wandsworth. A largely Nigerian Pentecostal church (a long-standing tenant at Grafton Square) was interested in the building, as was the Trinity Presbyterian Church of Ghana. Then, at the Southern Synod, a presentation on the needs of churches from eastern Europe and south India challenged the good stewardship of resources. 'We felt that God's mission would be better served if our tiny congregation stopped clinging to our sizeable buildings and released to one of these larger churches who would inevitably make better use of them. Meanwhile we would join up with St Andrew's and boost that congregation. The two URC congregations enthusiastically decided to unite.'[3]

The hope of the Clapham folk and the URC Southern Synod was that the building in Grafton Square might be passed on to the local congregation of the Trinity Presbyterian Church of Ghana but, sadly, because of the unwritten relationship of that church with the United Reformed Church, and because its local congregation had no formal links with the URC congregation whose building it was sharing, the Charity Commissioners refused permission for this act of Christian fellowship and insisted that the premises be sold to the highest bidder. Limits were placed for the sale of the site by the church's trust deed. This laid down strict terms limiting the use of the building to another church. It was purchased by Maranatha Ministries.

Their website states that:

> The Holy Spirit directed our Pastor Dr Frederick Mmieh to start Maranatha Ministries in October 1990 as a Prayer Fellowship (House Group), with eleven members. This fellowship was known as Christian Prayer Fellowship International (CPFI). CPFI meetings were held on a rotational basis in the homes of members. Members were taught the Word of God and they shared practical fellowship by breaking bread... In 1991, the name of the fellowship was changed to the current name, Maranatha Ministries, as directed by the Lord. Later that year the Maranatha Ministries held its first evangelistic crusade at the Clapham Youth Centre, and thanks to the Lord for the new members added to the ministry. Maranatha Ministries was registered as a Charity in 1996 and also became affiliated to the Evangelical Alliance and the International Ministerial Council of Great Britain.

The website also speaks of Maranatha Ministries Worldwide Centre, Grafton Square, London, SW4 0DE and states that:

> Maranatha Ministries is a non-profit making registered Charity affiliated with the Evangelical Alliance and the International Ministerial Council of Great Britain. Our vision is to nurture and equip an assembly of believers through the ministry of the Word of God. We emphasize the message of Salvation, Healing and Deliverance, thus equipping our members for World evangelism and Church planting. We currently have branches in Asia and the Caribbean.

Sadly, at the time of writing in 2012, the building in Grafton Square stands empty, though the informant was unable to supply any other details.

***

Thus the story of **Clapham Dissenters** moved across Clapham Common from Old Town to a new place for worship and a new beginning for witness. The last service in Grafton Square took place on 24 November 2002:

> ... with guests from other United Reformed Churches and local ecumenical partners. The service celebrated independence and the right of a congregation to make its own decisions – even to close and move on. We sang 'The Lord hath yet more light and truth to break forth from his word'; and processed out into the hall and the last person switched the lights off.

Endnotes

Chapter 2: Clapham, the Place

[1] '... a little book published in 1827' and quoted in John Battley's *Clapham Guide* (1935).

[2] Memorial Tablet on the wall of Holy Trinity Parish Church, Clapham.

Chapter 3: Gathering Together

[1] F. Reynolds Lovett, *A History of Clapham Congregational Church* (1912).

[2] Anthony à Wood, *Athenae Oxonienses* (a collection of notes on seventeenth-century Oxford alumni), quoted by F. Reynolds Lovett.

[3] D. Brunton and D. H. Pennington, *Members of the Long Parliament* (1954).

[4] A. G. Matthews, *Calamy Revised: Being a Revision of Edmund Calamy's Account of the Ministers and Others Ejected and Silenced, 1660–2* (1934).

[5] Edward E. Cleal and Thomas George Crippen, *The Story of Congregationalism in Surrey* (1908).

[6] Matthew Wren (1585–1667), master of Peterhouse, Cambridge (1625–34); chaplain to Charles I, who he accompanied to his Scottish coronation in 1633; bishop of Hereford (1634–5), Norwich (1635–8) and Ely (1638–67).

[7] Bishop Wren's 'Visitation Articles and Injunctions' issued to diocese parishes before his visits.

[8] Edmund Calamy, *The Nonconformist Memorial* (1795).

[9] *The Works of the Rev. William Bridge*, Vol. 4 (1845), p. 299.

[10] www.apuritansmind.com.

Chapter 4: Scattered!

1   *Calamy Revised: Being a Revision of Edmund Calamy's Account of the Ministers and Others Ejected and Silenced, 1660–2,* p. 86.

2   Act of Uniformity, 1662.

3   *A History of Clapham Congregational Church,* p. 40.

4   *Calendar of State Paper, Domestic 1664–5,* p. 539.

5   Ibid., p.86 (quoting S. Palmer's *Nonconformist Memorial II,* p. 415).

6   *Calamy Revised: Being a Revision of Edmund Calamy's Account of the Ministers and Others Ejected and Silenced, 1660–2.*

7   Middlesex Sessions Rolls, 1682.

8   *Alumni Cantabrigienses* (1922–53).

9   Erasmus Middleton, *Evangelical Biographies* (1807), p. 39.

10 *Calamy Revised: Being a Revision of Edmund Calamy's Account of the Ministers and Others Ejected and Silenced, 1660–2.*

Chapter 5: Settled!

1   F. Reynolds Lovett, *A History of Clapham Congregational Church* (1912).

2   *Calamy Revised: Being a Revision of Edmund Calamy's Account of the Ministers and Others Ejected and Silenced, 1660–2,* p. 447.

Chapter 6: Growing Church

1   Sir Jerom Murch, *A History of the Presbyterian and General Baptist Churches in the West of England* (1835).

2   An occasional paper of Clapham Antiquarian Society (February 1968) describes a 1760 pamphlet entitled *An Account of the Riots which were made at a Dissenting Meeting-House in Clapham in Surrey*: 'These took place on the last Thursday in 1759 and the first Thursday in 1760, when the door and interior of the Meeting House were badly damaged and the people "insulted, pelted and their lives endangered". The rioters were led by a church warden named Hubbard. Efforts to bring the culprits to justice proved ineffectual. This building had been registered with the Bishop of Winchester by one John Dolman, pastor of a Congregational church at Shad-Thames, Bermondsey. The congregation eventually formed the Baptist meeting on South Side in 1777.'

3   *Calamy Revised: Being a Revision of Edmund Calamy's Account of the Ministers and Others Ejected and Silenced, 1660–2,* p. 59.

4   William Coward was a wealthy eighteenth-century merchant living

in Walthamstow, London. He owned ships and a plantation in Jamaica, and was a churchman with strong Calvinistic beliefs. When he died in 1738, at the age of 90, his will reflected his support for three Dissenting academies, for churches and ministers' dependents fallen on hard times, and for the extension of the Christian Gospel. A trust was set up to continue the work he so generously funded in his own day. Grants were made available for the 'education and training of young men for the ministry of the Gospel, and for the support and service of churches in the interest of Christ among Protestant Dissenters.'

5   The Revd Dr Daniel Williams (*c.*1643 – 26 January 1716) was a British benefactor, minister and theologian. He is known for the legacy he left which led to the creation of Dr Williams' Library, a centre for research on English Dissenters in Bloomsbury, London.

6   R. Tudur Jones, *Congregationalism in England* (1962), p.181, quoting John Waddington, *Congregational History, 1700–1800*, p. 505.

7   Theodore Schroeder, *Free Speech Defined and Defended* (1919).

8   John Penry (Penri) born in 1583, son of Meredydd Penry, Cefn Brith, Llangammarch. Educated at Peterhouse, Cambridge (BA, 1584) and St Alban's Hall, Oxford (MA, 1586). He presented to Parliament in 1587 his *A Treatise concerning the Aequity of a Humble Supplication.* He was arrested and brought before the Court of High Commission, but released. He married Eleanor Godley of Northampton in 1588; and they had four daughters. He published other similar books and was believed to be involved in the publication of *Marprelate Letters*. He fled to Scotland in 1580, returning to London 1582. He was arrested and tried and found guilty under the Act of Uniformity. He was executed by hanging, 29 May 1593.

9   *The Gentleman's Magazine and Historical Chronicle*, Vol. 95, part 2 (1825).

10   Ibid.

11   Ibid.

12   William Scott, *Stourbridge and its Vicinity* (1832).

Chapter 7: The Minute Book of 1773

1   *A History of Clapham Congregational Church*, p. 18.

2   Ibid., p. 87.

Chapter 8: Consolidation

1   *A History of Clapham Congregational Church*, p. 93.

2   Roger Lee, born *c.*1776. Married Ann Harding, daughter of Joseph Tompkins. Probably worked in shipping. Governor of Mill Hill School. Had a large household, including a governess, butler, footman, cook and several maids. Died 13 March 1855.

3   William Esdaile, banker and print collector. Born 6 February 1758, son of Sir James Esdaile, of Great Gains, Essex, who was once Lord Mayor of London. Commercial education, bank clerk. Father founded Esdaile, Hammet & Co., of Lombard Street, and William joined that company. Married Elizabeth, daughter of Edward Jeffries, treasurer of St Thomas' Hospital; two sons and four daughters. William Esdaile's collection of marbles and paintings (including *Infant Christ* by Leonardo da Vinci) etc. were auctioned by Christie's in March 1838. Died in Clapham, 2 October 1837. A grandson married the daughter of Percy Bysshe Shelley in 1857. See *Oxford Dictionary of National Biography*.

4   E. Groves, *The Weymouth and Melcombe Regis New Guide* (1835).

5   William Bengo Collyer, born in Blackheath, Kent. Entered Homerton Academy at age of thirteen (studied theology, 1798–1800). Ordained to the ministry in 1801; Peckham, Surrey (1800–55); afternoon preacher at Salter's Hall (1813–14) and (1825–6).

6   www.wbcollyer.org/index

7   *The History of the London Missionary Society II*, p. 173; quoted by Lovett, p. 94.

8   *A History of Clapham Congregational Church*, p. 97.

9   Quoted in his obituary in the *Congregational Year Book*.

Chapter 9: Nonconformist Might

1   *Congregational Year Book* (1871), p. 101.

2   David W. Bebbington, *The Nonconformist Conscience: Chapel & Politics, 1870–1914* (1982), p. 87.

3   Ibid., pp. 104–6.

4   The church published *Service Book 1884, with Hymns* (1884).

5   Quoted in *J. Guinness Rogers: An Autobiography* (1903), p. 287.

6   According to John R. Battley, *Clapham Ever Old Yet Ever New* (1937), p. 41, 'From the balcony over the door of this house, Mr Gladstone once addressed a meeting, and in Dr Rogers' drawing room delivered the opening speech in his Home Rule for Ireland Campaign.'

7   *The Nonconformist Conscience: Chapel & Politics, 1870–1914*, p. 88.

8   Archibald Philip Primrose (1847–1929), 5th Earl of Rosebery. Under-Secretary of State (Scottish Affairs), 1881–3. In a speech in Australia, he coined the phrase 'Commonwealth of Nations'. Foreign Secretary 1886 and 1892 to 1894. Prime Minister, 1894–5. A Liberal Imperialist who advocated reform of the House of Lords. His horses won the Epsom Derby in 1895, 1904 and 1906. He owned twelve horses, which he kept at Durdans, Epsom, where he died in 1929.

9   *The Story of Congregationalism in Surrey.*

Chapter 10: The New Theology

1   John M. Drennan OBE DCM became a church member in 1919. He was a deacon (1926–57) and church treasurer (1935–47). He remained a member and a life deacon after moving to Deal. His 'An Old-timer Remembers' appeared in *Grafton News* in March 1968.

2   Elaine Kaye, *The History of Kings Weigh House Church* (1968), pp. 115–16.

Chapter 11: A Busy Church

1   The Penny Bank movement emerged in the late 1840s / early 1850s in an attempt to discourage the working classes from irresponsible use of hard-earned wages. It was supported by the Temperance movement of the time as a means of discouraging heavy drinking. Considerable numbers were founded in churches, chapels and clubs.

Chapter 12: Some Graftonians

1   Amelia Salt (1842–1914) married Henry Wright, builder of railway carriages. He was a deacon at Kensington Chapel, chairman of London Congregational Union (1880–1) and treasurer of the LMS, the London Chapel Building Society and the Coward Trust.

Chapter 13: Into all the World

1   Griffith John (1831–1912) was born in Swansea. He preached his first sermon at fourteen (at Ebeneser Welsh Independent Church) and two years later began to preach regularly. After training for the ministry at Memorial College, Brecon, and Bradford Academy, he was accepted for service with the LMS and began a two-year training course. He was then ordained at Ebeneser, Swansea, and married Margaret Jane, daughter of Madagascar missionary David Griffiths. He had thought of going to Madagascar himself but was

sent instead to China, where he and his wife arrived in September 1855. John was among the first missionaries in the three provinces of Hubei, Hunan and Sichuan. He became fluent in several spoken and written Chinese dialects, and became known as an author, translator and preacher. He travelled huge distances to proclaim the Gospel, founding schools, hospitals and colleges. His wife died in Singapore on a journey back to Britain in 1873. A year later he met and married Mrs Jenkins, the widow of a missionary, who returned with him to China. He became chairman of the Central China Tract Society and was a founder-member of the permanent committee for the Promotion of Anti-Opium Societies. Griffith John translated the New Testament, Proverbs and Psalms into Mandarin and published a Wen-Li New Testament as well as translating the New Testament and parts of the Old Testament into several other dialects. He founded the theological college which still bears his name in the Yangtze valley. In 1888/89 he was elected chairman of the Congregational Union of England and Wales but declined the honour, preferring to remain in China. Eventually, he returned to Britain in January 1912, but died in London on 25 July and was buried in Swansea. Edinburgh University had awarded him an honorary DD in 1889 but he died before being able to receive a similar honour from the University of Wales.

2   China refused to have dealings with the outside world until the early nineteenth century. This isolation was first broken by British trade in opium, which was banned in China. During the century the Chinese were forced to make concessions, including the opening up of ports and the acceptance of foreign embassies. Western-style reforms were introduced in the face of opposition from the masses. In 1900 there was a terrible drought and peasants faced ruin. They blamed foreigners and their gods. This discontent was seized upon by a secret society called the Sacred Harmony Fists, nicknamed the Boxers by Europeans, whose aim was to expel all foreigners from the country. With the encouragement of the Dowager Empress, ruler of China, attacks were made on foreigners, of whom some 250 were killed along with 30,000 Chinese Christians. A force of European, American and Japanese troops occupied Beijing and harsh peace terms were forced on the Chinese government.

Chapter 14: Strength and Weakness

1   *Clapham Observer*, 10 June 1932: 'It is of interest to note that Clapham Congregational Church is the only church of that denomination having a surplice male choir, consisting of some forty voices.'

2   G. Stanley Russell, *The Road Behind Me* (1936), p. 161.

3   G. Stanley Russell published *A Book of Public Worship* in 1955. The preface contains these words: 'If I were to adopt any form of dedication or to associate them with any interest in my life, it would be with the rich memories and deep affection that fill my heart, after more than twenty-five years of ministry in Deer Park, and with the equally fragrant fourteen years before that in Clapham Congregational Church, London, England, where such forms of Service first took shape in my mind, and were employed to some considerable extent.'

4   Pamela Hansford Johnson CBE (1912–81). Born in London, the daughter of Reginald Kenneth Johnson, colonial civil servant, and Amy Clotilda Howson, singer-actress. Educated at Clapham County Grammar School for Girls. She left school at sixteen to take a secretarial course and worked for several years at the Central Hanover Bank and Trust Company. She began writing poetry and then turned to prose. Among her published works were 27 novels, seven short plays, critical works and short stories and a memoir, *Important to Me* (1974). She and Dylan Thomas considered marriage but eventually abandoned the idea. She married Gordon Neil Stewart, an Australian journalist, in 1936; they had one son and one daughter. They divorced in 1949. She married the novelist C. P. Snow, Baron Snow, and had a son with him.

5   *The Road Behind Me*, p.177.

6   Ibid., p. 190.

7   Ibid., p. 24.

8   Draft letter from Fred. J. Ware.

9   Russell's letter dated 1 June 1929.

10   *The Road Behind Me*, p. 69.

11   Ibid., pp. 167–8.

12   Ibid., p. 176.

13   Ibid., p. 199.

14   Items in London Archives.

15   *The Straits Times*, 25 April 1930.

Chapter 16: Rising from the Ashes

1   Rachmanism is the exploitation and intimidation of tenants by landlords. Peter Rachman (1919–62) was a landlord in London who became notorious for unethical practices, including driving out tenants to maximize revenue from his rental properties.

2   Pauline Webb, Methodist lay preacher; officer of the British Methodist Overseas Division; vice-moderator of the World Council of Churches

Central Committee (1968–75); organiser of religious broadcasting, BBC World Service (1978–87); co-editor of the *Dictionary of the Ecumenical Movement* (1991); co-chair of the World Conference on Religion and Peace; president of the Society for the Ministry of Women in the Church. Her autobiography *Memories of a Life in the Universal Church* was published in 2006.

Chapter 18: Grand Finale

1   Letter from the Revd Ann Cole, 2 June 2011.
2   Letter from the Revd Alex Mabbs.
3   Ibid.

Further Reading

Clement Colman, *The Clapham Chant and Anthem Book* (1886).

R. Tudur Jones, *Congregationalism in England 1662–1962* (1962).

Edward W. Lewis, *The Unescapable Christ and other sermons* (1907).

Frederick Reynolds Lovett, *A History of the Clapham Congregational Church* (1912).

J. Guinness Rogers, *An Autobiography* (1903).

G. Stanley Russell, The *Monastery by the River* (1930).

G. Stanley Russell, *The Church in the Modern World* (1931).

G. Stanley Russell, *The Road Behind Me* (1936).

G. Stanley Russell, *A Book of Worship* (1955).

Phillip Simpson, *A Life of Gospel Peace, A Biography of Jeremiah Burroughs* (2011).

What we are doing at Grafton Square (1912).

Grafton News, the monthly magazine of Clapham Congregational / United Reformed Church (1907–2004).

Lovett's 'Modern Authorities'

Robert Barclay, *The Inner Life of the Religious Societies of the Commonwealth* (1879).

David Batten, *Clapham with its Common and Environs* (1841).

David Bogue and James Bennett, *History of Dissenters* (1810).

Browne, *History of Congregationalism in Norfolk and Suffolk* (1877).

Samuel Clark, *History of Nonconformity*, Vol. 1 (1911).

Edward E. Cleal, *Congregationalism in Surrey* (1908).

R. W. Dale, *History of English Congregationalism* (1907).

John William Grover, *Old Clapham* (1885).

John Stoughton, *Ecclesiastical History of England* (1867).

John Waddington, *Surrey Congregational History* (1866).

Lovett's 'Original Sources'

17th Century

Frank W. Bate, *The Indulgence of 1672* (1908).

William Bridge, *Sermons* in his *Collected Works* (1845).

Bridge and Burroughes with others, *The Apologetical Narration* (1643).

Edmund Calamy, *The Nonconformist's Memorial* (1702), edit. S. Palmer (1802).

Daniel Neal, *History of the Puritans* (early 18th century).

Robert de Montjoie Rudolf, *Clapham Before 1700* (1904).

Lyon Turner, *Original Records of Early Nonconformity under Persecution and Indulgence*, 2 vols (1911).

Anthony à Wood, *Athenae Oxonienses* (1674).

18th Century

Philip Furneaux, 'Works', especially, *Letters to Mr Justice Blackstone* (1771).

Edward Grace, *Sermons on the death of Mrs Crisp* (1701) *and Mr Crisp* (1703).

Walter D. Jeremy, *Presbyterian Fund* (1885).

Moses Lowman, 'Works', especially – *Case of the Acts against the Protestant Dissenters* (1712); *Principles of an Occasional Conformist Stated and Defended* (1718); *Dissertation of the Civil Government of the Hebrews* (1740).

Walter Wilson, *History of Dissenting Churches in London* (1910).

Articles in *Protestant Dissenting Magazine* (1798); *Gentleman's Magazine* (1807); *Monthly Repository* (1807).

19th Century

Walter D. Jeremy, *Presbyterian Fund* (1885).

Richard Lovett, *History of the London Missionary Society 1795–1895* (1899).

J. Guinness Rogers, *The Gospel in the Epistles* (1897).

20th–21st Centuries

Leslie Artingstall: *Towards a Christian Economic* (1942).

E. W. Lewis: *New God and Other Essays*; *An Expression of the New Theology*.

G. Stanley Russell, *The Face of God and Other Sermons* (1935).